The Turmoil at Talangsari

A Splinter of the Darul Islam Movement

W. Wasis

The Turmoil at Talangsari

A Splinter of the Darul Islam Movement

With an Introduction by Ramadhan K.H.

Balai Pustaka
Jakarta, 2003

State Publisher House
BALAI PUSTAKA

BP No. 5714

First edition October 2003

297.8
Was
t

Wasis, W.
The Turmoil at Talangsari : A Splinter of the Darul Islam Movement / W. Wasis. – Pub. 1 – Jakarta: Balai Pustaka, 2003.
xxvi, 258 hlm. ; 20 cm. - (Seri BP no. 5714).

1. Islam - Aliran 2. Talangsari - Tragedi
3. Darul Islam
I. Judul II. Seri.

ISBN 979–690–029–7

Design cover : **Adjie Soesanto**
Layout : **Gatot A.S. & Abdulrahman**

PREFACE

THIS work is the result of field research conducted by Widjiono Wasis which, according to Ramadhan K.H., has a unique, unconventional, and direct style not often seen in books that delve into similar episodes.

The author has expended much time and effort into his research. Though not always a smooth process, it has finally resulted in the successful publication of this book.

Particularly interesting is the conclusion of this work, which explores the concept of reconciliation as the basis for settling all forms of disputes in order to achieve peace and unity and avoid social fragmentation. Toward this end, we hope that this book makes a significant contribution.

Balai Pustaka

LOCATION OF THE TALANGSARI 1989

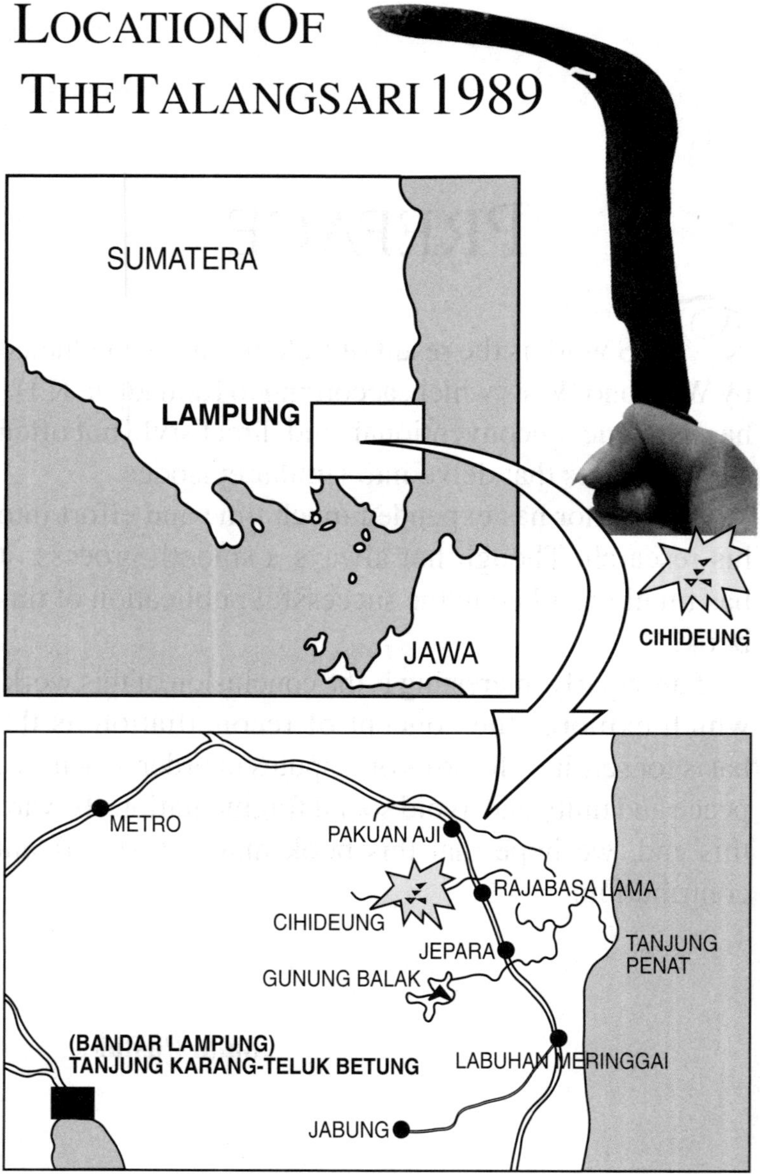

INTRODUCTION BY RAMADHAN K.H.

An Opinion

A recent acquaintance, Widjiono Wasis, presented me a draft of this text. It grabbed my attention, leading me to read it very thoroughly. He titled the text "The Turmoil at Talangsari, A Splinter of the Darul Islam Movement."

In February 1989, a great tragedy occurred in Cihideung, Lampung. During this event, a group of district-level officials was attacked and Captain Soetiman was killed. Following from this, there was a physical clash as locals and security authorities joined forces against those who had killed the state official. Among the latter, a person by the name of Warsidi became the focus of attention by all quarters. In the end, Warsidi was shot dead; a number of other persons also became casualties, though the exact number remains unclear.

Wasis has delved deep into this tragedy. As he mentioned to me, he was drawn to this topic because of the strong opposing viewpoints that surround the case. There are certain parties that want to uncover and question the events behind this incident. According to Wasis, however, the local community has expressly avoided comment to these interest groups. Moreover, he says, the Talangsari upheaval has unique characteristics relating to the history of the Islamic struggle in Indonesia.

Wasis was inspired to research this tragedy as it relates to religious beliefs. In looking at it from that perspective, we will be reminded how it relates to the Darul Islam movement, the Indonesian Islamic State (*Negara Islam Indonesia*, or NII) concept, and to the ideologies of influential figures and events that have been linked to these, such as S.M. Kartosoewiryo, Daud Beureuh, Ibnu Hakar, Kahar Muzakkar, the 1981 Cicendo incident, the 1981 Woyla hijacking, and the Tanjung Priok tragedy.

Wasis worked for almost one year to arrive at a narrative that he sees as reasonable and which he feels can be presented to the public. He began work in May 2000 and finished in April 2001; this included a two-month field trip to Lampung, research at libraries and other archives, and another three months to edit the results. He has paid much attention to contemporary histories, including biographies and autobiographies, as well as extensive oral interviews. On top of that, he brings his own extensive background to the subject.

It should be mentioned that his other published works include *Ensiklopedi Nusantara* (PT Dian Rakyat, 1989) and *Almanak Jagad Raya* (PT Dian Rakyat, 1992). While in a separate field, no less impressive are his *Kamus Bisnis* (PT Dian Rakyat, 1994) and *Ensiklopedi Pelajar* (PT Dian Rakyat, 1995).

***

I am far from expert in the topics covered by this young researcher. Still, his diligent field research has attracted the attention of the public, myself included. Its composition and style is unconventional and direct—not often found in books that delve into similar incidents. His knowledge of Islam is beyond reproach, including the concept of reconciliation in conflict resolution. Lastly, I was driven to comment on this work following a statement from retired Lieutenant General A.M. Hendropriyono, who as a colonel was touched by this incident when he was commander of the *Black Garuda* military region in Lampung. The general pointed out to me that the data obtained by Wasis was indeed factual. I note that A.M. Hendropriyono has never stopped expanding his educational horizons, and for him to make such a comment is powerful because it means putting his reputation as an intellectual at stake.

***

Following his field research and oral interviews, Wasis has concluded that the Talangsari incident was not a rebellion. The Warsidi group was not a separatist movement like the contemporary ones (as of 2001) in Aceh, Maluku, or Irian Jaya. It was also not a misguided sect. Too, the Warsidi group was not planning a *coup d'etat*; Wasis found no signs of any coup intentions. They did not seek to equip themselves with weapons similar to those carried by the military. Rather, Wasis believes the group was a movement intent on disrupting the peace by creating large-scale riots, this after feeling guilt over killing a military official from the local area.

The research conducted by Wasis took considerable time and effort. The hardest and most rewarding part, he says, was to track down former followers of Warsidi, the central figure in this incident in Lampung twelve years ago. While this research is commendable, research into the Lampung tragedy should not stop at this point. Hopefully, contributions from other researchers will follow.

Ramadhan K.H.

Jakarta, 5 June 2001

CONTENTS

ACKNOWLEDGEMENTS

WITHOUT the assistance of many parties, publication of this book would not have been possible. By the time I had completed the draft, I fully realized that it was the compilation of efforts by many persons, many names, many powers.

Because of this, I would like to express my gratitude to all of you who have, either directly or indirectly, contributed to the publication of *The Turmoil at Talangsari*. Among others, this includes Lukman Hakim Gayo, Usman Yatim, Sugiono M.P., Miryul Miron, Achman Azhari, and Zulkarnain Bahri.

First and foremost, I would like to express my sincere thanks to one person who was intimately involved in the making of this book—and even deserves credit for coming up with the idea in the first place. He, too, sourced funds when I needed them for timely publication. He is Achmad Yani Wahid.

Further thanks go out to a number of sincere persons, including Colonel Mudjiono (Lampung), Zulkifli Maliki (Lampung), Widagdo Hadi Mahksum (Lampung), Widi

Yarmanto (*Gatra*), Kelik Nugroho (*Tempo*), and many others too numerous to mention. Last but not least, thanks go out to my family for their clear vision and open heart in helping me see completion of this work.

Whatever assistance all of you have given, no matter how small, it is now a part of this book. It is my hope that the result is worthy and valuable.

The Author

Jakarta, 20 May 2001

A Note on Names

When it comes to names, one should not be careless. This belief is grounded in religion. When God decided to create a prophet on Earth, name was an issue. Angels are also subject to the power of names.

Having a name is an honor. Adam became honorable because he mastered names. Names are knowledge. They are of foremost importance, before all the powers of human knowledge.

This not only pertains to creatures. Even God had an undefined number of names. It is known that he had more than 200 beautiful names. Therefore, the Messenger of God appreciates parents who give their children beautiful names, and will certainly not love persons who mistreat names.

This book cannot avoid mentioning names. Indeed, a number of names are contained in these pages. The possibility of incorrect or incomplete spelling is very high. If this is the case, it was not done intentionally.

May God forgive me. I would like to apologize in advance; please accept my best intentions.***

FORWARD

IN the past, there have been many incidents of unrest. Especially when related to politics, even if there is a small spark, people will begin to shout and it is certain that some Muslims will revolt. This is a fact. Especially after several incidents appeared in a row, it appeared as if they were a coordinated series of events.

In looking back over a series of such upheavals, there has been speculation that they were related. The 1984 Tanjung Priok tragedy, for example, has been tied to the 1989 Talangsari incident. There have been further linkages of incidents over a wide range of locations. For example, the 1981 Cidendo Bandung incident, the 1981 Woyla hijacking, the Haurkoneng incident, and the events inspired by Warman (who died in 1981) have been viewed by some as parts of the same extended unrest.

Such speculation, however, seems far from the truth. After all, these events do not seem directly linked to each other. Each of these incidents has different central figures. The root causes also seem unrelated. The Tanjung Priok tragedy, for example, was centered around a character known as Amir Biki. This differs from the Talangsari event, which featured Warsidi.

Concerning the Tanjung Priok riot, it might be better to refer to it as a disaster rather than a tragedy as members of a religious community sought to struggle. It followed no planned scenario with a beginning and an end. Rather, this incident occurred spontaneously and escalated abruptly. If heroes or victims emerged form this tragedy, that is another issue. By contrast, the Cicendo and Imron cases had different characteristics. Both of these were protest movements against policy; they chose to express themselves by extraordinary means, like hijacking an aircraft.

The Lampung incident was not a protest movement, nor was it a spontaneous event. It was far different from the Cicendo, Imron, and Tanjung Priok events. It also differed from the Haurkoneng unrest. The Warman movement, which sought to spread terror anytime and anywhere, was also different. Lampung had some characteristics in common with all of these. The events themselves, the locale, the main figures, and its historical background all came together in a planned and systematic manner.

At Lampung, there was a commotion. There was uncontrolled greed. There was a band of persons who did not understand that "when Earth is stepped upon, there is a sky overhead." In Lampung, there was an assassination. There was a link between Warsidi and the NII concept. There was a link between them and a place called Ngruki in Solo. That is not all. There was also an aim by a group of persons to realize their dream of establishing an austere commune as a base for their struggle. And from the Lampung incident, there has emerged a move toward reconciliation among the opposing parties. What is unique is the fact that this path toward reconciliation came from those who caused the commotion in the first place.

These are the complexities and nuances that are the background to this book, and why it is now in your hands.

Regarding Numbers

This book presents my findings about the many issues surrounding the 1989 Lampung incident. Perhaps the most interesting aspect about the Lampung case regards the number of casualties, including both fatalities and survivors. Who killed them? How were they killed? What were the weapons used? Who are the witnesses? When were casualties inflicted? People want answers to these questions and many more.

When certain persons cited figures for the number of Talangsari casualties, some in the mass media grabbed these numbers. Nobody critically asked where the numbers came from, how they were obtained, and what criteria were used.

Arriving at the number of casualties is not a problem provided that the finding is supported by facts, data, and sound reasoning. Unfortunately, some of the numbers issued to the public about the number of victims at Talangsari have not only misled the public, but also the victims themselves. Moreover, some of the numbers have been intentionally falsified to smear certain persons or parties. Most recently, there have even been news stories about persons who have intentionally profited from the issue.

In the end, it was found that the confusion over the number of victims stemmed from a person who arrived at the number after reviewing a press release. Using intuitive reasoning, he deduced a figure and then passed this to several local media outlets. From the local media, public opinion was formed. In time, it became a public truth.

The question over the number of victims ultimately became a hotly debated issue for the local community, who did not see the hundreds of alleged fatalities from the incident in their area. Surviving eyewitnesses have expressed doubt and now believe the false reporting had a political element. The local community has correctly pointed out that they know more about Talangsari than anybody else. Anybody who wants the real story about the Talangsari incident should contact them in order to get the right facts.

The local community has also stated that there have been persons who reported on Talangsari and gave casualty statistics without ever coming there, much less having met with the community. They regret such conduct because, in addition to opening old wounds, it continues to impede their region. According to one source, Talangsari has become an object for the personal benefit of a group of persons.

The complex issues surrounding the Talangsari incident still attract much public attention, especially during the present time when transparency is a must. These days, incidents like the upheaval at Talangsari will always be scrutinized by a generation in search of a more perfect time.

My journey to Talangsari took place for the reasons I described above. A number of locals who claimed to be eyewitnesses to these past events were interviewed and have revealed much about the unrest. I not only met with members of the community, but also with former members of the Warsidi group who were responsible for the uprising. They spoke openly without any effort to hinder my research.

From the testimony of these two sides, much can be deduced. For example, we can get a good idea about the size of the Warsidi group. We can accurately gauge the number of fatalities and survivors. We can understand why the conflict took place. We can understand more about Warsidi and his links to the NII. All of these issues were discussed directly and thoroughly with the interviewed sources.

Urban Myths and Rural Realities

It is interesting to note that during my field research, I found many differences between opinions in the cities and realities in the rural setting where the upheaval actually took place. Many things that went unreported in the media could be found in the countryside. For example, perceptions as to whether Warsidi is seen as a hero or an oppressor became more clear. According to some in the city, Warsidi is a courteous farmer and respected teacher of the Koran.

Concerning the involvement of government officials in this incident, the local community clearly stated that they saw the role of the authorities as public protector. Had the authorities not acted promptly, locals find it hard to imagine what might have taken place. This is because Warsidi did not want to compromise with local leaders, who he had branded as infidels. Warsidi had also irrationally killed a local official (Soetiman) that was looking into events in the vicinity. This farm laborer and teacher of the Koran was like a small king who did not know about the rules of village life. The local community admits that they were scared and intimidated during the time he was there.

Those officials who succeeded in countering Warsidi's uprising are held in very high regard by the locals, despite the fact that they have been vilified by the urban community and international media. This dichotomy motivated me to investigate the Talangsari turmoil, and flesh it out into a book. It is these opposing viewpoints that will color the contents of this work.

A Refusal to Speak

The local community at Talangsari has long refused to discuss its old wounds, wounds that have been a source of prolonged social trauma for their region. Toward non-government organizations (NGOs) that want to delve into the Talangsari incident, the locals have expressly kept them at a distance. This is because they see more disadvantages than advantages in talking to them. The NGOs use humanitarian concerns as a mask, but actually have no humane intentions underneath.

The locals, too, well know that they will be sold out by those groups calling themselves NGOs. They especially abhor the reprehensible behavior of several NGOs that have profited from the Talangsari incident overseas.

This book certainly does not want to be trapped into describing only the superficial aspects of the Talangsari unrest. The background to the Talangsari upheaval must be exposed. This includes the close correlation between Talangsari, the NII, and the Darul Islam movement.

For this reason, several parts of this book detail the NII movement that was driven by, among others, S.M. Kartosoewiryo, Daud Beureuh, Ibnu Hajar, Kahar

Muzakkar, and others who have been given the dishonorable title of rebel. We still need to know why they rebelled and why they had their outbursts. It seems like such unrest is constantly flaring in this country, especially when political disputes are shaped by narrow interests.

In Lampung, the turmoil had characteristics that were unique and not seen in the earlier episodes of unrest. The Central Lampung (currently East Lampung) unrest has something else that was unique: a means of successfully resolving the problem. Those involved in the issue made use of the Islamic concept of *islah*, or reconciliation. In the last chapter of this book, all aspects—from A to Z—about reconciliation are discussed in brief.

Enjoy your read.***

1

DUSK IN CENTRAL LAMPUNG

LAMPUNG, 1989. It is a rice bowl, a food warehouse for Sumatra and its surroundings. It is blessed with fertile soil for its dwellers. Not just rice, but also sugarcane, tobacco, rubber, cocoa, vanilla bean, and more. Historically, it was also been famed for its pepper; this spice was a top commodity for the European markets.

When the Portuguese occupied Malaka in 1511, the race for Lampung's black pepper was on. Disputes and quarrels became unavoidable. This simple black condiment caused hostilities to break out among nations. In Lampung, the Portuguese battled on a daily basis. Tension got progressively worse, until finally a major war broke out. This war lasted for two years from 1518 to 1520. The people of Lampung, with the assistance of Palembang, came out on top. Portugal retreated in a daze. From that point onward, the European powers were no longer interested in coming to that pepper-producing region on the edge of Sumatra.

Following from this period, trade ties between Lampung and Palembang developed, but were later hindered by interference from the sultanate of Banten. The sultanates of Banten and Palembang never had a good relationship. The developing pepper trade with Europe caused these two sultanates to lose their sound reasoning. They forgot the religious teachings from their ancestors. Lampung, meantime, had a vested interest in both of the disputing sultanates.

Hundreds of years ago, Banten and Lampung were one unified region. At that time, Java and Sumatra were not divided by the legendary eruption of Mount Krakatau. It was after that eruption that the Sunda Strait separated the two lands. Still, the relationship between Banten and Lampung endured. Many Bantenese moved to Lampung to begin farming in its open, dry paddy fields. The influence of the Banten sultanate over Lampung continued to increase, especially after Banten ruler Fatahillah married Princess Sinar Alam, a daughter of the Queen of Pugong (presently the Jabung region of Central Lampung).

From this marriage, a son was born named Hurairi. He was later named Haji Muhammad Zaka Waliullah Rau Darah Putih, and nicknamed Minak Kejala Ratu. He was later founder of the Darah Putih kingdom based in Kauripan (which includes Penengahan sub-district in Central Lampung), and was an ancestor of the wellknown Lampung hero, **Raden Intan**.

During the Banten-Palembang war of 1596-1608, Lampung's interests straddled the two sides. As two pepper producers, with a key market in Palembang, good ties between Lampung and Palembang were indispensable. However, the marriage between Princess Sinar Alam and Fatahilah, the Banten ruler, could not be broken. The dilemma was resolved when Banten attacked Palembang. The Banten-Lampung marriage of royals seems to have had a political purpose for Fatahillah: to get the support of Lampung.

For a long time, the Banten sultanate had been worrying that Palembang would take over Lampung's pepper trade. In fact, Palembang had long been one of the pepper ports for South Sumatra, Jambi, and Bangka. It was also anticipated that Palembang would expand its reach to include the pepper from Tulang Bawang in Lampung. If this proved the case, it would be dangerous for Banten because Lampung had been the best supplier of pepper to Banten for European consumption.

To export this product, Banten's port had become one of the most important trading outposts in the western part of the archipelago. European and Asian traders marketed their goods at this port and, when going home, brought with them such products as black pepper, white pepper, nutmeg, ginger, and other spices.

Meanwhile, the Dutch East Indies Company (known by the initials VOC) dropped anchor in the Lampung Strait to monitor the spice trade from there. The VOC had long targeted Lampung's black gold.

Their first ship had docked there and occupied Sebesi Island on 23 August 1624. It did not last long due to crew unrest and disease, which forced the ship to leave port. Not until 1661 did the Dutch return with two large ships, dropping anchor in the Semangka Strait.

The VOC had good reason not to dock at Banten and trade from that port. The pepper price at Banten at that time was 15 *reals*, whereas the purchase price in Lampung was just 7-9 *reals*. Because of this, traders preferred to bypass Banten and anchor in Lampung.

However, direct trading with Lampung was not too easy. The long-established influence of the Banten sultanate was a major obstruction. Moreover, after Sultan Ageng Tirtayasa came to power in Banten, ties between Lampung and Banten became inseparable. It certainly complicated things for the Dutch and prevented them from controlling Lampung. The Dutch eventually came to believe that they would not be able to control Lampung without overthrowing Banten first, especially after their request to establish a small port in Lampung was rejected by Sultan Ageng Tirtayasa. After that rejection, the Dutch sought revenge against the Bantenese ruler.

From Banten, there came news of a conflict between Tirtayasa and Sultan Haji, his own son. The Dutch immediately sought an audience with Sultan Haji and encouraged him to seize power. This prompted the sinful son to act. With the assistance of the Dutch, he killed his father. After the death of Sultan Ageng Tirtayasa, he appointed himself sultan of Banten.

As a reward, the VOC obtained a monopoly over the pepper trade. From that point forward, Lampung—the homeland of Raden Intan—was explored and exploited by the VOC, then the English, then the Dutch once more until the Japanese occupied the territory in 1942. During this period, the plight of the farmers and despair of the local population always tinged Lampung.

The Struggle of Raden Intan

Once upon a time, there was a legendary struggle by Raden Intan and his decedents. As the King of Negararatu in nearby Kalianda, he refused to abide by the Dutch. Raden was an aristocrat and descendent of Fatahillah, the founder of Banten. Because he could not sit idle while his land was subjugated, he rebelled and declared war.

Again and again, battles broke out. Casualties fell on both sides. There were battles everywhere. The locals left their hoes and sickles and took up all sorts of weapons. Rice fields were neglected. The harvest produced nothing. Not only did the farmers lose out, but also the Dutch. In the end, the Dutch offered to negotiate. Raden Intan's power was to be restored, and he was even offered a pension from the Dutch.

For the sake of his people, Raden appeared to accept the Dutch offer. But setting an example, the king—who went by the title Dalom Kusuma Ratu IV—never betrayed the true interests of his community. While giving the impression of being cooperative, he was actually secretly planning several uprisings. Such duplicity did not last for long. The Dutch were not easily fooled, and they soon detected the prince's ruse. They immediately ordered troops to arrest Raden, who happened to be ill at the time. After pretending to surrender, the king of Negararatu requested that the Dutch soldiers take a rest. As they slept, he ordered his troops to set up an ambush. On 13 December 1825, they struck. In the subsequent battle, the commander of the Dutch troops, Lilievre, was killed. The operation to arrest Raden Intan I was a total failure.

Three years later, in 1828, Raden Intan I died. He was replaced by his own son, Raden Iamb II, nicknamed Kusuma Ratu. Raden Iamb continued his father's rebellious ways. This young king successfully influenced other royals and sultans to struggle against the Dutch. The Dutch, in return, felt threatened. Dubois, a high-ranking local colonial official, wrote a letter to the governor general recommending that the tribal heads in Lampung be eliminated and Raden Iamb II be arrested.

In 1832, a warship and three cruisers with 300 Dutch troops, assisted by 100 prisoners, attacked Lampung. The raid proved fruitless; even Captain

Hoffman, the commander, was killed. The Dutch were incensed. Impatient, they conducted a second attack with a larger strike force. However, the results were equally disappointing. The Dutch returned to their barracks empty-handed and Raden Iamb remained free.

The Dutch continued to brood. Finally, on 25 September 1834, they launched a third attack. This time, the operation was led by Colonel Lout and 21 experienced officers. The Dutch also used 800 special soldiers equipped with heavier weapons. Large and small cannons were brought forward to kill the young king of Negararatu. After a month, they successfully captured the defenses at Raja Gear; Raden Iamb II, however, was able to escape by turning to the king of Lingam. Unfortunately, the king of Lingam proved to be a Dutch sympathizer and handed Raden Iamb over to the colonial authorities. Raden Iamb was brought to Batavia, then banished to Timor island until his death in 1838.

Even though the Dutch had been successful in killing their hero, the fighting spirit of the Lampung people never died. A son of Raden Iamb II continued the jihad against the Dutch. This crown prince was later enthroned as Raden Intan II. He then initiated a long war between the Dutch and people of Lampung through 1856, at which time leadership was passed to the next generation.

During the course of the long war, on 5 October 1856, Raden Intan II accepted an invitation to meet

Raden Ngerapat. Together with one of his followers, he was ambushed by Raden Ngerapat and was killed with honor. His corpse was immediately brought before Minister Colonel Wilson. Two well known Islamic religious teachers were called to confirm his identity. Yes sir, they said, this is Raden Intan.

Even though their leader had been taken, the people were still enthusiastic to perpetuate a guerrilla war. Like a wind that blows through the hinterland, they sprung up in various villages to continue the fight. Still, their resistance was futile against the trained ranks of the Dutch military. But while every uprising was quickly quelled, the colonial government never ruled in peace in this spice-producing land.

Not until 1890, when the situation in Lampung was deemed extremely safe, did the Dutch open the area to mass plantations. A half century later, the Japanese came and pushed this colonizing power out, which ultimately led to Indonesia's independence.

Dusk in Central Lampung

Nineteen years after Indonesian independence, on 18 March 1964, Lampung became a separate province. Its provincial symbol incorporates a paddy and peppers (natural products), a machete and spear (traditional weapons), a gong (democracy), a slice of open fruit (cultural majesty), and an opened umbrella (shelter), all of which are set on a shield. The last symbol—the umbrella—refers to the fact that anyone can come and seek shelter and get protection in Lampung, a reflection of its population of both indigenous people and recent migrants. For this reason, the motto of the province is *Sang Bumi Ruwa Jurai*.

The first governor of Lampung, Kusno Danu Upoyo, was only in office for two years (1964–66). He was succeeded by Zainal Abidin Pagaralam (1966–73), R. Sutiyoso (1973–78), Yasir Hadibrata (1978–88), and Poedjono Pranyoto. Only one year after Poedjono took office, a tumultuous event took place at the foot of the province's Mount Balak. Specifically, it took place at Cihideung village at the hamlet known as Talangsari III in Way Jepara sub-district of Central Lampung.

Central Lampung district covers 9,189.5 square kilometers. Its capital is Metro, which is a food center for the entire province. Over 60 percent of all consumable goods needed in the province are supplied by Central Lampung. In addition to its rice paddies and farmland, the mountainous area of Waja and Sukadana in Central Lampung have considerable iron deposits. Inevitably, many people came to this edge of Sumatra to seek a living. This area attracted the attention of many low-income Javanese, who came there because they had no money and their own agricultural land was of poor quality and in short supply.

Therefore, Lampung is not just a rice basket. It is also an area that takes in many newcomers who are either running from something or because they are economic migrants. In coming to Lampung, they are free from the law and debt. What they get from Lampung's spice and crop-producing areas is far better than what they left behind. Migrants from Java, in particular, began to skyrocket. In 1922, there were 5,500 migrants from Java. Eight years later, the number had reached 33,000. In this rural area of Sumatra, which is still inhabited by Sumatran elephants, the flood from Java continued unimpeded. Central Lampung was first opened to cultivation in 1935, especially around Metro. By 1941, there were more newcomers working this land than natives.

The success of these migrants in this sugar-producing area led the Indonesian central government to continue its transmigration policy. Initially, this caused a dispute between the central authorities and the indigenous people. This is because the central government placed their own people into power—in the form of bureaucrats—who displaced the role of traditional leaders. This angered many community leaders, who noted that even the Dutch had taken their traditions into consideration. Why did Jakarta limit traditions? A simmering feud began. This conflict came to a head on 20 December 1956, when the indigenous people of Sukadana near Way Jepara, Central Lampung, submitted a complaint to the government. Finally, in 1959, the central government answered by refusing to recognize the existence of the traditional leadership. The situation grew more heated. The government's stance belied its support of the highly successful transmigration program, which in effect was a continuation of colonialization.

At the time, the central government was extremely weak. Its cabinet changed frequently. The NII and its armed insurgents—namely, the *Tentara Islam Indonesia* (TII) and Darul Islam—were rapidly growing in several areas. The government attempted to crush these rebels. However, there were fears that demobilized troops might join forces with the rebels that had a strong influence in Jakarta and West Java.

In order to prevent the demobilized troops from joining with Darul Islam/TII, the government created a program called the National Reconstruction Bureau. To supervise it, the ministry of defense formed a National Reserve Corps that included active-duty military officers. Most of the members of this corps were sent to isolated areas in South Sumatra; their aim was to both become pioneers in development and to bolster local security.

In reality, the results in the field deviated from the plan. As a result, the government was forced to take a number of steps. In 1956, Central Lampung was declared off limits for transmigration. The reason given was because it was already too densely populated.

Still, Javanese who were drawn by the earlier success of transmigration secretly entered the forests of Lampung. One of the target areas of these illegal migrants was the forests around Mount Balak, which were considered especially fertile. Since 1960, about 20,000 hectares of this nature preserve were cultivated by about 100 newcomers who came to populate 13 villages by the end of that decade.

Efforts by the government to replant this area and resettle these 'muhajirin' proved futile. These people did not want to move. They were ready to die for the sake of defending the land they had cultivated. They would defend any plot of land to the death. When village administrators came, they instinctively drew their swords. A signal drum would then be sounded, *Ono rojo pati, ono rojo pati!* A killing has taken place! The news spread fast. A killing has occurred!

In the end, the provincial government felt it necessary to accommodate the aspirations of the illegal settlers, as they had contributed to the revenue of the region. The 13 villages populated by unofficial transmigrants were properly recognized as regular villages. The incumbent governor of Lampung, R. Sutiyoso, issued a decree on the establishment of the Gunung Balak sub-district and legalized the new villages in 1974.

Later this decree came under review. It was even revoked following a water crisis that swept through Lampung. The water reservoir at Way Jepara became very low as a result of poor water retention after an excessive amount of trees in the nature reserve were cut down. This water was supposed to feed an irrigation program for 22,000 hectares of rice paddies. Reforestation was now seen as a must, and the illegal dwellers had to be resettled either voluntarily or involuntarily.

After difficult negotiations, the settlers at Gunung Balak agreed to move to North Lampung. This was realized after mobilizing the armed forces, which helped prepare new land in 1986. However, about 1,000 families insisted on staying in order to collect their harvest. But several harvests later, they still had not left. On the contrary, the Gunung Balak vicinity, which was supposed to be empty, continued to receive new settlers. The number climbed ever higher.

The government was left with no alternative. The settlers had ignored repeated warnings to leave. On 19 November 1988, an operation was conducted involving ten officers. Huts had to be demolished and their dwellers forcibly evicted. Those who resisted were arrested. When necessary, huts had to be burned down. There were about 100 settlements that were subject to this operation.

From that point forward, the Gunung Balak sub-district was not officially recognized. It was excluded from administrative maps of Lampung. Officials continued to pressure the community. As soon as they put up huts, they were taken down. This led locals to look for revenge. Why did the authorities oppose the country people? Therefore, when somebody came and shouted that the government was tyrannical and Pancasila was invalid, the people welcomed it enthusiastically.

There was a dark cloud over Central Lampung. Children did not run around and laugh. Mothers did not spend their customary time chatting with each other at dusk. On the contrary, gloom was pervasive. Turmoil could occur at any time. Songs of misery were sung. Cheerfulness was rare, taken away by the setting sun. This was the picture of Central Lampung's Cihdeung as of mid-1989.***

Important Events in History

1511: The Portuguese control Malaysia. Sumatra was their next target, and they are set to compete for Lampung's black gold, which was popular in Europe. This product, black pepper, brings both happiness and misery, smiles and tears.

1518: The Portuguese arrive. The ruler of Lampung is disliked. Battles occur. The war lasts until 1520.

1596: The situation in Lampung is confusing. There is fighting between Palembang and Banten. The Lampung area at the bottom of Sumatra is torn between these two competing interests. As a pepper-producing area, it has market interests in Palembang. Lampung, therefore, must maintain good ties with Palembang. But its relations with Banten can not be neglected, especially after Princess Sinar Alam, the daughter of the Queen of Pugong (in Central Lampung) marries Fatahillah, the sultan who founded Banten. This dilemma comes to a head when Banten attacks Palembang (1596-1608), and, due to the pull of the sultan following his marriage to the princess, Lampung is forced to side with Banten. On 12 June, a VOC ship anchors in the Lampung Strait.

1624: On 23 August, the VOC occupy Besi Island and Sebesi Island. This does not last long. Riots and disease force the Dutch to depart both islands in their ships in 1625.

1661: From 22 June to 10 July, two VOC vessels enter the Semangka Strait and anchor there. This was to compete for trading routes, and to monitor the political situation in the local area.

1682: The VOC secures a trade monopoly in Lampung on behalf of Sultan Haji, the new ruler of Banten. Sultan Haji seized power from Tirtayasa, his father, on the encouragement of the Dutch. This betrayal was fully backed by the Dutch. This coup d'etat in Banten has an impact on Lampung's future. On 29 June, a VOC expedition from Betawi left for Lampung; after stopping in Banten between 8-24 August, it arrived in Lampung on 29 August.

1732: Lampung enters a new era when the sultan of Banten dies.

1751: Bandits frequently come to Lampung from Johor, Bugis, and Mandar. Because of this, the area remains unsafe until 1800.

1808: On 22 November, a decree is issued making Lampung fall directly under the Dutch governor rather than Banten or the VOC. Locals led by Pangeran Indra Kusuma resist in Abung (Kota Bumi) and cannot be quelled.

1812: Lampung falls under British control because Banten and Java are surrendered to England by the Dutch.

1816: Lampung reverts to Dutch control because England lost a war in Europe. Lampung is placed under the Banten resident; from there, Assistant Resident Krisman runs the local administration. However, King Raden Intan of Negarataru (in nearby Kalianda) mobilizes forces against the Dutch. Raden Intan is a descendent of Fatahillah.

1817: A settlement is reached after the sovereignty of Raden Intan I is recognized by the Dutch and he is given a pension from the colonial authorities. The negotiation breaks down, however, and the Dutch become irate.

1825: The Dutch send troops to Negararatu with the intention of arresting Raden Intan I who was also known as Dalom Kusuma Ratu IV. At the time, he was ill. He asked the Dutch to grant him two days for him to go to Telukbetung along with a colonial escort. This request was approved, and the party traveled as far as Negararatu before taking a rest. On 13 December, Raden Intan I and his followers attacked their Dutch escorts. The leader of the Dutch troops, Lelievre, was killed and Lieutenant Misonius injured. The arrest attempt had failed. Three years later, Raden Intan I dies, and was replaced by his son, Raden lamb II (who was given the title Kesuma Ratu). Anti-Dutch sentiment became more apparent. Kesuma Ratu grew more popular, and expanded his ties to other kinds and Bugis sailors. The Dutch grew restless.

1832: The Dutch conduct a fresh attack with a warship, three cruisers, 300 Dutch troops, and 100 Bugis soldiers. The operational commander, Captain Hoffman, was again unable to succeed. He was injured in this battle and died.

1834: A second Dutch attack also fails. A third attack under the command of Colonel Lout (on 25 September) makes use of 21 officers, 800 special soldiers equipped with large cannons. This latest attack succeeds in occupying the Raja Gear defenses on 24 October. Raden lamb II escapes to Lingam and asks for help. However, the king of Lingam surrenders him to the Dutch. Raden lamb II was sent to Betawi and then banished to Timor island until his death.

1850: The son of Raden lamb II is enthroned as Raden Intan II by K.H. Wakhya of Banten. His struggle against the Dutch intensifies. The war continues until 1853.

1853: An agreement between the Dutch and Raden Intan II is concluded.

1855: The Dutch raze Lampung because Raden Intan II did not live up to the 1853 settlement. Brutal fighting lasts through the middle of 1856.

1856: On 10 August, the Dutch set anchor in the Tanjung Tua strait at Sikepal Island. Two days later, an ultimatum is sent to Raden Intan II to surrender. He ignores the warning. When Raden Intan II does not leave his base, the Dutch attack. This battle lasts through 5 October. Raden Intan II was betrayed by his own followers. He was arrested when he went for negotiations with the Dutch.

1890: The Dutch open Lampung for mass plantations.

1929: Lampung becomes an *afeling* headed by a resident. Anti-Dutch sentiment subsides.

1942: The Japanese arrive. The Dutch are expelled and go back to their homeland.

1945: On 17 August, Indonesia—including Lampung—proclaims its independence.

1956: A tense situation in Central Lampung unfolds when the indigenous people of Sukadana send a letter of protest to Jakarta demanding that the central government recognizes their local customs and leadership. Central Lampung is declared off limits for transmigrants.

1960: The fertile Gunung Balak area is exploited by illegal migrants. This ultimately becomes a prolonged problem.

1964: On 18 March, Lampung celebrates when it becomes a province. The first governor, Kusno Danu Upoyo, stays in office for two years.

1974: The problematic Gunung Balak vicinity is named a sub-district. This is codified by a gubernatorial degree that was hastily issued by R. Sutiyoso. He later revoked his own decree.

1988: On 19 November, an operation is conducted to drive out the illegal community at Gunung Salak. Nobody physically resisted, but those that were evicted were incensed because their belongings were lost and homes razed.

1989: On 6 February, misery came to Central Lampung at the Talangsari III hamlet in Rajabasa Lama village of the Way Jepara sub-district. This was perpetrated by a group of individuals armed with machetes, swords, and arrows. They vented their anger against the government and Pancasila. They were known as a strange and aloof group who had previously taken crops without permission. When officials came to ask for an explanation, they were attacked. Captain Soetiman, the commander of the outpost at Way Jepara, was brutally killed. A full-blown confrontation ensued. Many people were killed. The turmoil in Central Lampung left behind misery and several valuable lessons.

2

THE HISTORY OF TALANGSARI III

IN the cosmology of traditional Javanese puppet theater, there is a concept of *Amarta*. This refers to a prosperous, peaceful, and rich country. In this place, the people live comfortably. Everything is available and easy to obtain without much difficulty. The people are afforded protection not only from their ruler, but also from the surrounding environment.

When this author was still a child, *amarta* described Java, its people, and its social conditions. Though it is a relatively simplistic view, it was apt for those who knew about Javanese puppetry as children.

Perhaps *amarta* referred to a Java of the past. The current Java is different. Many of its people have crossed borders, some even going to other countries. For them, they have abandoned Java because it is no longer a prosperous, peaceful, and rich place. Java is only a past memory for those that have left it.

Sukidi, 40, may not be a representative of the Java of the past. Today, he is a resident of Lampung. He left Java 28 years ago as a participant in the transmigration program. Now, he earns a relatively good income compared with his past life in Java, which offered him little hope. Now in Talangsari III hamlet in Way Jepara sub-district of Central Lampung, Sukidi has relatively high standing. He has even been appointed as a community leader.

With high hopes, Sukidi had departed Banyuwangi, East Java, for Lampung. The year was 1972, when Lampung did not yet have that many transmigrants. Sukidi went against the norm: instead of abiding by the common Javanese motto "Whether or not we have something to eat, we must live together," he followed "Whether or not we live together, we must have something to eat." With great enthusiasm, he went to Way Jepara, leaving behind his friends and relatives.

Way Jepara is one of 23 sub-districts in Central Lampung. As of the 1989 census, it covers an area of 240 square kilometers comprising 20 villages with 80,000 occupants. Of the 20 villages, one of them is Rajabasa Lama. Within Rajabasa Lama village, there is a small hamlet known as Talangsari III. This hamlet of just 40 hectares would be all but unknown had it not been for the crimes and uprising against the government that took place there. It is difficult to believe, but it is true.

Clearing the Jungle

When Sukidi came in 1972, Way Jepara was not like it is now. At that time, Way Jepara was a jungle largely untouched by human beings. Much of its was forested, making it a good place to hunt animals. Changing a jungle into a village is not easy. Only certain qualified people can do it successfully.

After he found a good location for a settlement, Sukidi was among those that cleared the forest around Talangsari. He had chosen an area full of durian trees, which he thought would make a good area for a village. According to Sukidi, the area was ideal because there was reddish soil rather than the soil with a high sand content that was common around Lampung.

The native from Banyuwangi then tried to look for the original landowner in the area. From the village office, he got news that Amir Puspa Mega, the chief of Rajabasa Lama village who was known to have many inherited properties in the vicinity, was the rightful owner. From that point forward, Amir Puspa and Sukidi worked together to clear the virgin land.

Together with Sudjarwo and Ngatidjan, two of Sukidi's friends, they pushed back the forest to make a settlement area. Small and big trees were cut. Part of the land was chosen for houses, and the other part for farmland. In the history of Talangsari, these three people are considered to be the village founders. The area was subsequently named the Talangsari III hamlet.

Cihideung

Clearing the forest is not easy. Only a hard worker with a clear vision can accomplish the task. Not everybody has such an ability. This is not just an isolated story: there have been many accounts of those that have succeeded, and many accounts of those that have failed.

The story of Cihideung, the village that bordered Talangsari, is interesting. Prior to the time that Sukidi cleared away the durian trees around Talangsari, there was another group of people that wanted to make a settlement there. However, without any clear reason, they abandoned the land after they gave it the name *Cihideung*. It is rumored that they came from the Sundanese area of West Java.

Others in the vicinity later tried to clear Cihideung, but they also failed and left the area. Around two years later, Sukidi worked hard to strip away the durian trees and finally succeeded in opening Cihideung. After their success, they continued using the same name of Cihideung. One of the original occupants was the family of Jayus, who hailed from Sukidi's hometown of Banyuwangi.

Opening the land like this was a common practice for Javanese coming to Lampung. This was advantageous for both sides. The original landowners were happy because their land now had some economic value and could be used as productive farmland or orchards. It could then be resold for a higher price than virgin land.

For those that worked the land, they also got a profit. They could work on the land as if it were their own property, without actually having to buy it. They only had to share the results of the harvest if the land actually produced anything.

This was the experience of Sukidi and his friends. They even had a chance to purchase the land they cleared. Amir Puspa Mega offered Sukidi the chance to buy the land in installments, according to his ability. In this way, Sukidi could obtain several hectares of his dreamland. Amir Puspa's land actually amounted to about 25 hectares, with 6 hectares set aside for Sukidi and his friends; it was the latter that became known as Talangsari III.

In order to get the land, Sukidi joined with his friends and purchased it as a joint venture. For example, if one hectare of land cost Rp 30,000, they collected money from 30 persons. That meant that one person only had to provide Rp 1,000. The land would not be divided right away; rather, they would wait until additional areas were purchased and recorded in Sukidi's register.

Amir Puspa had what was considered good land. The soil was blackish-red in color, not sandy. Land with sandy soil was sold at a cheaper price of around Rp 10,000 per hectare. For Sukidi, it was not easy to earmark some of his money for land purchases. At the time, all the locals found it difficult to live. They had barely enough for meals.

Sukidi and his friends went from village to village to work as day laborers in order to collect funds. They worked for three days as day laborers, while the other four days were spent working Amir Puspa's land. If they received Rp 100, some was saved and the rest was spent on daily necessities, such as buying kerosene and dried cassava. Dried cassava was a basic food item for them.

Food from Cassava

For Sukidi, dishes made from cassava were a main menu item. It was a source of energy for his daily life. Rice combined with dried cassava was called *nasi uleng*. It is very simple to make: cassava is soaked in water, then grated into a powder and dried. This powder is cooked with beans and some rice to give it taste.

Sukidi's other friends generally followed this way of life. Initially, he only had three people in his group. Twenty-eight years later, that number has risen to more than 100 heads of households.

Changing Boundaries

This story is really a tale of two villages—Rajabasa Lama and Pelabuhan Ratu—changing their boundaries. Why is that? There was a hamlet that belonged to Rajabasa Lama, but it was actually closer to Pelabuhan Ratu village. On the other hand, there was the hamlet that belonged to Pelabuhan Ratu, but it was closer to the territory of Rajabasa Lama.

The hamlet of Umbul Kacang, which is listed as part of Rajabasa Lama village, is about 25 kilometers from the village center. This makes it closer to Pelabuhan Ratu village. If an official wants to visit Umbul Kacang, he or she must pass through several areas controlled by Pelabuhan Ratu. On the other hand, Pelabuhan Ratu also has an area under its jurisdiction that was very far from the village office. This was the area known as Cihideung hamlet, which bordered Sukidi's settlement in Rajabasa Lama village.

As a result of these far locations, village officials had difficulty visiting their own hamlets. To facilitate administration and supervision, the leaders in both villages agreed to exchange the areas. This agreement was signed in July 1988. Umbul Kacang came under the control of Pelabuhan Ratu and Cihideung came under the control of Rajabasa Lama.

Cihideung and Sukidi's settlement were adjacent, and share a border with each other. The Rajabasa Lama community subsequently conducted negotiations and agreed to join the two areas into one. These two areas were thus merged into what became known as Talangsari III.

Talangsari III

If Amir Puspa Mega, who was indigenous to Lampung, did not fight to use the name Talangsari for the area south of the provincial road crossing, it is highly likely that the area would have been given a name taken from the area around Banyuwangi. It was rather common for new settlers to Lampung to bring the names of their old villages to their new settlements.

As a result, it is not strange to find villages in Lampung sounding like relocated Javanese villages—the new settlers not only brought themselves, but their home villages as well. In Lampung, for example, there are areas named Pekalongan, Blambangan, Sukohardjo, and Wonosobo; in Central Lampung, there is a district named Surabaya. Some day there might even be a village named Jakarta.

Talangsari III was the name given at the request of Amir Puspa Mega when he was village chief. For the people of Lampung, the words *talang* and *umbul* are not new. There are several other areas named umbul—for example, Umbul Puk and Umbul Hujan Mas in Pakuan Aji. There might even be further uses of this name that are not registered.

In the case when families establish a commune of five or six huts within a village, this cluster is usually called an *umbul*. When more than one umbul are gathered, they automatically become a *talang*. A group of talang is called a *dusun* (hamlet). Talangsari III was the third hamlet in the immediate area; Talangsari I and Talangsari II had already been in existence before Sukidi cleared away the durian trees belonging to Amir Puspa Mega.

Talangsari was actually a merger of two hamlets from adjoining villages. The hamlet covered about 40 hectares and was shaped like a small island. It was surrounded by the narrow Beringin River, which encircled the best cocoa producing field in the area. To get onto the island, five bridges spanned the two and a half meter width of the river. These bridges were later all destroyed by Warsidi's gang to prevent the authorities from coming.

As it turned out, the merger of the two hamlets had taken place just four months before the turmoil broke out. Administratively, the merger caused no problems. But socially, it caused considerable problems for some people, who lost some of their rights when they had to join under Talangsari III. The area now came under the control of Sukidi, who was considered a rather low-class citizen; this might have been the trigger that caused Warsidi to ignore Sukidi when he came to ask for their identity documentation.

As the hamlet chief, Sukidi had no choice but to carry out his job. He arranged the administrative data for the hamlet, including census information, land titles, and other data such as the registration of Warsidi and his group.

After two or three months of trying to fulfill his duties, Sukidi began to encounter disturbances and opposition. He was made aware of several strange occurrences. Increasingly, Warsidi and his men were becoming aloof and hostile. Sukidi, in turn, was concerned that Warsidi was growing uncontrollable. Tensions flared. In their chest, they were beginning to feel hatred and condemnation.***

POETRY OF TURMOIL

There is turmoil in the people's farmland.
There is upheaval among them.
Their property is lost.
Stalks of bamboo fly away.
In a different time, a different day,
Some people say
They have lost their coconuts.
This is not a lie.
Some people say
They have lost their cassava.

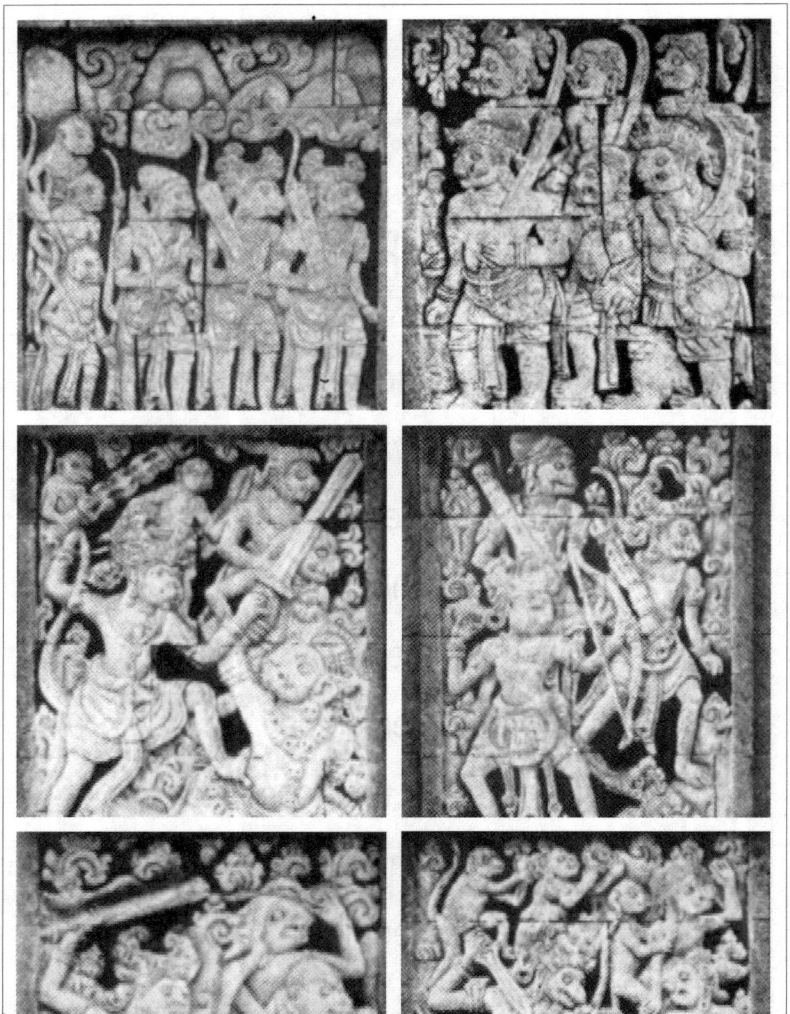

3

THE TURMOIL AT TALANGSARI

FOR Sukidi, the hamlet chief of Talangsari III, Way Jepara, Central Lampung, the group of mysterious visitors were making his life difficult. They were extremely rude, not offering the customary greetings normally given by guests. Moreover, they seemed intent to stay for the long term.

Feeling slighted, Sukidi reprimanded the leader of the visitors. The response he got was not what he was looking for. On Earth, it is only God that we must follow, said the visitor. When Sukidi asked for his name, he was variously told **War, Anwar, Warsidi,** or **Anwar Warsidi**—the appointed leader of the ***Jama'ah Mujahiddin Fisabilillah*** Group.

A Small Group

Warsidi's group in Talangsari had historical links to a second small group in Jakarta. It is said that those who established the Jakarta group were Nurhidayat, Ahmad Fauzi, Wahidin, and Sudarsono. They were teens who enthusiastically studied religion, then felt disillusioned when they saw that Indonesian law was not based on Islam.

They felt that their nation and country was being deceived. Islamic law must be implemented, they felt. But How? First, they had to come together to pray. Then they had to pray to mobilize their power into a strong binding spirit. They had to become like a tree with firm roots in the ground, which cannot be upended by a big or small typhoon.

From their solidarity in prayer, they then wanted to build a Muslim commune where they could be free from intervention by deceitful authorities. There they could establish religious order. This was the start of a big dream: to build the NII long advocated by supporters and sympathizers.

To realize this dream, the Jakarta group envisioned three stages. First, they declared all persons outside their group to be infidels. In other words, those that did not follow the law of God were infidels. This even included high clerics: if they were unwilling to apply Islamic law, then their blood was to be considered unclean. Second, they rejected Pancasila as their ideology. This is because the government had made the people stray from Islamic rule by its imposition of Pancasila. Third, they fasted in 40-day intervals, worshiping and praying together to make their souls ready to be saved.

For those that had completed these three stages, they were entitled to move to Lampung to join Warsidi. From this group, the name *Jama'ah Mujahiddin Fisabilillah* was born. And they were also the one that would later perpetrate a bloody upheaval.

Warsidi Loses Control

After joining with the Jakarta group, Warsidi's voice grew louder. Members of the local community describe how Warsidi and his entourage increasingly became uncontrollable. Their speech was fired with hostility, opposition toward the government, and condemnation of Pancasila. The authorities were infidels, corrupted by money. Therefore, they prohibited civil servants from receiving salaries. And they refused to pay taxes, even though it was an obligation.

On one occasion, Sukidi asked them to work with other locals to build a road through the village. In response, they said that the Koran did not teach people to work together. When Sukidi asked them to protect the environment, he received a similar response. Because of this, other locals began to question their principles, especially their propensity to steal crops.

From that time forward, communal unrest became evident. Locals carried out their daily activities with anxiety and fear, especially after several of Warsidi's followers came to Sukidi's house bearing machetes and swords. Signs of imminent conflict became more apparent. Several locals fled their plots of land and became refugees. This included Sukidi's family, who moved to a neighboring hamlet to escape the terror from the commune.

Reflecting over the situation, Sukidi realized he no longer had any power. He immediately reported this to his superior, Rajabasa Lama village chief Amir Puspa Mega. Together, Sukidi and Amir Puspa Mega reported the matter of Warsidi's disruptive actions to the sub-district authorities in Way Jepara. The yelling from Warsidi's gang was gradually being heard—even to the point of reaching foreign countries.

The cries from Talangsari grew louder still. The turmoil left sorrow in its wake, not only for Warsidi and his followers, but also for all the other villagers. This sorrow has continued to the present.

***

CHRONOLOGY OF THE TURMOIL THE DEATH OF CAPTAIN SOETIMAN

THERE was an uprising in the people's farmland. Some people are causing unrest. Property is lost. Stalks of bamboo fly away. There were even reports of coconuts and cassava being stolen.

These issues were brought to the attention of Sukidi. As the hamlet chief, he could not let this take place. Sukidi conducted an investigation, opening his eyes and ears. He got news that there were visitors at Jayus's house; they had odd behavior that went against tradition, including a propensity to take other people's crops without permission. These odd events were the opening acts in the drama of the Talangsari III unrest.

The hamlet chief went to visit and investigate Jayus's house. He found the reports correct: there were indeed visitors there who did not have any clear origin. When he asked them about their identity, they were evasive. When they were questioned about the missing community crops, one said that the Earth belongs to God, and that anybody had the right to enjoys its products. Such statements became the basis for trouble not only with the government authorities, but also with the local community.

The following is a chronology of the events that led up to the disaster. It is intentionally described in detail in order to give an exact picture of the occurrences that have had such a tremendous impact on the political situation in Indonesia. These details may not be well known to many people, especially since many "facts" that have been spread until now do not match with the realities on the ground.

This account is based on true facts and on data collected in the field, which has been taken from first-person sources both in the form of oral interviews and original documents.

CHRONOLOGY

Wednesday, 11 January 1989

1. Sukidi and Mansur sent a letter to Amir Puspa Mega. It states that at 2000 hours on the previous Thursday night, Jayus, a citizen of Cihideung, received fifteen visitors from Jakarta. These visitors consisted of both men and women.
2. The visitors wanted to conduct a Koran study session on Friday, led by a cleric named Pak War. The newcomers did not have any identity cards and did not report themselves to the local authorities.
3. They said that on the following Friday, they would invite other visitors from Malaysia.

Thursday, 11 January 1989

1. Based on Sukidi's report, at 1000 Amir Puspa Mega sent a letter to Zulkifli Maliki, the Way Jepara sub-district chief, about the Cihideung situation. The letter from Sukidi was enclosed.
2. At 1130 hours, Zukifli send a letter to village chief Amir Puspa Mega ordering Jayus, Pak War, Mansur, and Sukidi to the Way Jepara sub-district office. In the letter, Zukilfi asked Amir to immediately stop and prohibit any Koran activities that involved visitors from outside,

especially without any permit from the local authorities.

3. At 1630, after receiving the letter from the sub-district chief, Warsidi immediately prepared a typed response. The contents read:

> ***To the Chief of Way Jepara sub-district***
>
> *Dear Sir,*
>
> *After reading your letter and understanding its contents, it should be known that we are very busy fulfilling our activities in studying the Koran. Therefore, we cannot come to your office. We are Muslims who believe in the religious verse that says the best government comes from the clerics, and the best clerics come from the government. Therefore, we are waiting for your visit to our commune to see the real situation. Waiting for your acknowledgement, may God bless you.*
>
> *Best regards,*
>
> *War*

4. Zulkifli admits that he felt like he was being slapped in the face when he read Warsidi's letter requesting that he come to the commune rather than Warsidi coming to the sub-district office. He was greatly surprised to get a response like that.

Friday, 13 January 1989

1. At 1500 hours, Zukifli decides to go to the commune. He takes the village chiefs from Rajabasa Lama and Labuhan Ratu, along with the hamlet chiefs from Talangsari III and Kelahang, and some other staff.
2. At the meeting, Zulkifli asks about the meaning of the religious verse quoted in the letter. Cleric War did not immediately respond. After turning to his left and right, his followers merely nodded their head. It was stated in scripture, Warsidi later stated.
3. Zulkifli stated that the one-hour meeting at the commune was strained and unfriendly. According to him, there were about 30 persons in the location. From the rear, he heard someone say, "Kill the sub-district chief!"
4. Before taking his leave, Zulkifli invited Warsidi to meet him at the sub-district office. War promised to go there on Saturday, 14 January 1989

Saturday, 14 January 1989

1. In the morning, Zulkifli waited for the arrival of War from Cihideung. He waited through late afternoon, but Warsidi did not come.
2. War had broken his promise not just on this occasion, but forever.

Tuesday, 17 January 1989

1. There were reports from the Al Islam boarding school in Labuhan Ratu I village that someone named Usman was causing unrest. A teacher from this school had chased away Kiai Junaidi, the owner of the school who had once helped him.
2. From a secret letter penned by Usman, it is discovered that he was linked to Warsidi.
3. Usman, a native of Semarang who was born on 13 September 1960, had a long history of opposition to the government. In 1985, he was sentenced to one year in prison at the Sleman District Court in Yogyakarta for slandering President Soeharto.
4. When he was being sentenced, he said, "I have no faith in this court. In the court of God, it will be seen who is right."
5. After serving his sentence, Usman disappeared. It was later known that he was staying at the Al Islam boarding school, which he seized from Kiai Junaidi.
6. Along with other leaders from the Al Islam boarding school, the village chief from Labuhan Ratu I reported Usman to the Way Jepara sub-district office.

Friday, 27 January 1989

1. Ten days after reading the letter from the Al Islam boarding school, Zulkifli passed the report to Captain Soetiman, the commander of the military sub-district command in Way Jepara.
2. In his report, Zulkifli asked Soetiman to immediately investigate Usman, and to summon both Jayus and Anwar Warsidi, the leaders of the Mujahiddin group from Cihideung.
3. Zulkifli also mentioned that he had previously summoned Jayus and Warsidi, but they refused to come. They had even threatened him when he went with a delegation to their base.

Saturday, 28 January 1989

1. When he received Zulkifli's report, Captain Soetiman was upset. He immediately wrote a letter of summons to Usman, Warsidi, and Jayus.
2. In his letter, Captain Soetiman gave them a deadline of Wednesday, 1 February 1989. However, Warsidi did not come.

Wednesday, 1 February 1989

1. Amir Puspa Mega, the chief of Rajabasa Lama village, sent a report to Soetiman on Warsidi's activities.
2. According to Amir Puspa Mega, Warsidi and his followers had performed strange acts, such as

learning to shoot arrows, practicing martial arts, and making bombs from empty bottles.

Thursday, 2 February 1989

1. The information from the village chief was reported by Captain Soetiman to the military district post at Metro, the capital of Central Lampung. From the military district chief, Soetiman is ordered to monitor the situation.
2. Without being seen, Sukidi quietly watched the commune. From behind bushes, he saw strange activities, such as teenagers wearing black uniforms and headbands wielding swords, machetes, and arrows.

Sunday, 5 February 1989

1. Soetiman decides to act promptly so as not to lose momentum. He immediately orders two of his subordinates, Sergeant Dahlan and Corporal A. Rahman, to go to the location.
2. These two representatives make contact with local village and hamlet officials, including Baheram, Sukidi, Poniran, and Supar.
3. That night at 2330 hours, they quietly approached the location and arrested six teenaged suspects (one of them later escaped). Among these suspects, they found a bag of arrows, five machetes, two swords, and two Molotov cocktails.

4. The suspects were Sardan bin Sakip (15), Mujiono bin Sadik (15), Parman bin Bejo (19), Sidik bin Japar (16), and Saroko bin Basir (16). Sadar, alias Joko, escaped when they were brought to the sub-district office.
5. These teenagers originally came from Bandar Agung and Labuhan Maringgai in Central Lampung, with the exception of Saroko, who hailed from Teluk Betung.
6. After the authorities were unable to get any information from the suspects, they transferred them from the sub-district office to the military sub-district post. The authorities at the military sub-district were also unable to gain any information from them, as they all refused to speak.
7. All of the suspects were transferred to Military Region Command 043 in Bandar Lampung.

Monday, 6 February 1989

1. At 0100 in the morning, Warsidi is surprised to learn that some of his followers have been arrested. He orders Fadhillah to release them by force. That night, Fadhillah and twelve others depart on this mission. They are armed with machetes, swords, and Molotov cocktails. They run through the forest for several kilometers to make their way to the military sub-district post at Way Jepara.

2. At 0600 in the morning, Fadhillah and his band arrive at their destination. Before they launch their rescue, they learn that the suspects have been transferred to the military region command in Bandar Lampung. Fadhilah consults with his group and they agree to continue their trip to Bandar Lampung. Before departure, however, they go to Sidorejo in order to stop by Zamzuri's house to rest and map out their action. From Zamzuri's house in Sodorejo, they plan to raid Bandar Lampung that afternoon.
3. At 1100, the chief of the military district at Metro, Major E.O. Sinaga, takes a delegation to Rajabasa Lama sub-district in order to meet with Warsidi. From the Rajabasa Lama sub-district office, the military district chief's group is led by Captain Soetiman toward Warsidi's house, which is about 7 kilometers away. They are divided into three groups: the military sub-district chief's group, the military district chief's group, and a third group comprised of district officials. Captain Soetiman is on a motorcycle and is in front, followed by a jeep with the military district chief, and another jeep with sub-district chief Zulkifli and village officials.
4. At 1130 hours, the groups approach the location. They find the area quiet, as if it were deserted.

From afar, they heard the sound of Captain Soetiman's motorcycle being turned off. After that, they heard someone scream, 'God is Great!,' after which arrows were fired from the bush toward Soetiman. Dozens of members of Warsidi's group emerge from bamboo huts and attack Soetiman's group. Major Sinaga, who was shocked by the assault, yelled for his people to retreat. Sinaga's vehicle smashed through trees in order to get away. This was in contrast to Soetiman, who was injured and tried to flee, but received a fatal cut to his neck from behind.

5. At 1230, in Jayus's small mosque, Warsidi's followers debated their course of action. They began to argue, as the followers were torn about what to do next after killing an official. Not all of the group agreed with this action. Those who opposed the killing began to flee in all directions toward Pakuan Aji, Talangsari, and Kelahang. As they arrived, the local communities saw fear in their faces caused by the killing of the official. In the course of this exodus, Warsidi sent a delegation to find Fadhillah and tell him to immediately return to Cihideung.
6. At 1530, after prayers, the body of Soetiman was buried. Fadhillah came to meet Warsidi. According to Fadhillah, Warsidi ordered them

to change their strategy after realizing that Soetiman was dead. Fadhillah was now ordered to create chaos throughout Lampung in order to keep the officials busy and not focused against Cihideung. Late that afternoon, Fadhillah went to Sidorejo to meet his group and brief them about their changed mission.

7. At 1930, Fadhillah and his group depart on their new mission. In their own minds, they are convinced that they are doing what God wants. From Zamzuri's house in Sidorejo, they intend to go to the Military Region Command in Bandar Lampung. They traveled from Sribawono to Panjang, a distance of about 90 kilometers. To expedite their trip, they rented a car. Unfortunately, a member of the armed forces, Private Budi Waluyo, joined them for the ride. On the way, they introduced each other, and Budi Waluyo admited that he participated on the mission to the Cihideung commune. Haring this, an angered Fadhillah stabbed Budi Waluyo in the chest and killed him. Seeing the murder, the driver fled the car. Fadhillah and his group continued the trip, with the intention of reaching their destination by morning.
8. At 2000, while Fadhillah was heading on his mission, officials look to reclaim Soetiman's

body by force after receiving no signs of surrender from Warsidi.

Tuesday, 7 February 1989

1. At 0100 hours, a special forces team goes to monitor the location.
2. At 0300, an officer warns Warsidi through a megaphone to surrender the body of Soetiman. There are no signs that Warsidi's group is prepared to compromise. They seem to be ignoring the warnings. As morning comes, someone hidden from sight gives the order to launch a jihad. Warsidi's followers then emerge with arrows and machetes to attack the authorities. The authorities intend to meet the challenge.
3. At 0700, Loso (60) and Kamarudin (30), both residents of Pakuan Aji who are acting as guides for the authorities, hear cries from a hut at the commune. They look to see where the cries are coming from. They then discover that Warsidi's people are killing those from within their own group that want to surrender. Kamarudin even saw a member of Warsidi's group set fire to one of the huts.
4. At 1130, the fire at Warsidi's house is brought under control.

5. Now, eleven years later, the Talangsari III community is again disturbed by people wishing to open old wounds. Community leaders and officials from boarding schools in Central Lampung suspect that new players acting behind the front of humanitarian organizations are looking to defend Warsidi. Crimes and the truth are becoming blurred.***

4

About Anwar Warsidi

IN principle, there is no such thing as a bad or evil person. Man, after all, is the light of God, and God is always perfect and good. That said, when somebody lets his or her heart grow empty, the devil will fill the void. The contents of one's heart will determine whether he or she is an angel or a demon.

That is why the Almighty, who is King over all things on Earth, always asks us to remember Him—so that evil elements will not have a chance to take over the heart.

Whether or not the person in question here—Warsidi—allowed his heart to grow empty of God's light is not an easy question to answer. But we can get a good indication one way or the other from those who were close to him. On the one hand, there are those who cite his goodness. But others point to his weaknesses. Pulling together stories from various parties, including many that have thus far gone unreported, will allow us to get a more complete story of controversial leader **Anwar Warsidi.**

Testimony of Marsudi

Marsudi, 65, might be one of the best sources of information on Warsidi. This is because he is Warsidi's blood brother, one of nine siblings born to the same father, Marto Prawiro. Of the nine siblings, only Marsudi remained in close contact with Warsidi. Even until Warsidi's death, Marsudi was at his side.

The age of the two brothers was close, with only four years separating them. Though Marsudi was older, Warsidi was far more mature. Warsidi, too, exhibited patience and other good characteristics. Since childhood, Marsudi recalls that Warsidi was loved and trusted by friends. He was also known as a diligent and hard worker.

Warsidi received a formal education only through elementary school. After that, he only studied the Koran under a village cleric named Kiai Sirot. From Kiai Sirot, both brothers received a good foundation in religious principles. With such knowledge, they went to Lampung. Their sister, Maryumi, had already gone there as part of the transmigration program. In Lampung, too, was Maryumi's brother Marjudi (aka Muhammad Judi), who had gone there as a migrant in 1939.

The youngest child, Warsidi, was born in 1939 in a small village named Sebrang Rowo, near the Borobudur temple in Magelang district, Central Java. His siblings included Marjudi, Maryumi, Marsandi, Marsiyah, Marsidi, Marsudi, Suwandi, and Dulbahri. The two younger brothers, Suwandi and Dulbahri, passed away before the family moved to Central Lampung.

It is said that Maryumi was estranged from her brother Warsidi. This was allegedly because Warsidi became erratic after studying under a cleric named Anwaruddin. He reportedly even called Maryumi an infidel after she told him to stop studying under Anwaruddin.

According to Wardidi, Anwaruddin was a great cleric with deep knowledge. Warsidi believed that all people needed to be committed to his words. As a result, Warsidi was determined to follow Anwaruddin wherever the cleric took him. Since that time, the sister and brother had no further contact.

Since 1965, Anwaruddin had taught the Koran at Bandarjaya and Batanghari in Lampung. Warsidi first met the cleric after studying at a mosque in Bandarjaya. While praying, Warsidi caught sight of another man completing his prayers. He seemed extremely pious. After introducing himself, Warsidi quickly came to the conclusion that Anwaruddin was not an ordinary person. This was confirmed when

Anwaruddin went on to describe his life story to Warsidi.

Though having just met, Warsidi decided to become a student of the cleric. He followed Anwaruddin's every edict, including statements about killing infidels. According to Anwaruddin, killing an infidel is not a sin, and to fight them is a just Holy War (*jihad*). According to the cleric, the Indonesian government was comprised of infidels.

Warsidi took on more knowledge and principles from his teacher. For example, he was taught that secular governments must be replaced by Islamic states. Those who do not join with them and do not conduct themselves according to Islamic ways are infidels. At that point, the cleric's teachings were cut short when he was arrested and imprisoned for insulting President Sukarno.

Fortunately for Anwaruddin, he was soon released before trial because of the turmoil after the attempted PKI coup in September 1965. Sprung from jail, he was hounded out of his former community because his speech and behavior made the locals uneasy. He subsequently ran to Kogan Lima in North Lampung. Following his teacher, Warsidi and wife Juwariah also went there. With only a handful of supplies that he purchased after selling a plot of land, Warsidi lived alongside his fugitive teacher. At that point, he was far away from all of his siblings except for Marsudi.

After a year on the run, Anwaruddin passed away. Warsidi moved to take his place, even becoming a husband to his teacher's widow. To show his connection to the cleric, he changed his name to Anwar Warsidi.

Following Anwaruddin's death, Warsidi moved to Pakuan Aji. But due to bad economic conditions, the community was unwilling to accept Warsidi and his family. Not welcome in Pakuan Aji, he moved to Labuhan Ratu to work as a farmer while at the same time teaching the Koran to the local community. There he met Jayus, who then brought him to Cihideung.

When moving to Cihideung, Warsidi took along Marsudi, his only brother who showed empathy. With Marsudi, they began building a place intended as a commune for Islamic studies on land granted by Jayus. Before it was completed, however, turmoil destroyed his goal before his dream was realized.

A Story from Pakuan Aji

There is a revealing anecdote about Warsidi from Pakuan Aji, the village where he briefly paused before moving to Labuhan Ratu. The village chief from Pakuan Aji, 42-year-old Ismed Inonu, was a Lampung native born in that village. At the time Warsidi began preaching at Cihideung, Ismed was earning a living shuttling people back and forth from Talangsari on his motorcycle. Warsidi's location could only be reached by the road from Pakuan Aji.

As a Javanese who was well known in Lampung, Warsidi was a familiar figure to Ismed. According to Ismed, Warsidi blew into Pakuan Aji like a strong wind—and without any permission. He would come in fast, and disappear just as fast. Not reporting his arrival was his trademark.

The community had come to know him for the first time in 1987 when he stayed in the vicinity at Umbul Puk, an area still within the village boundary of Pakuan Aji. After that, Warsidi moved to Umbil Hujan Mas, where he worked on Marsan's pepper farm on a profit-sharing basis.

From Marsan, Ismed Inonu heard a strange story about Anwar Warsidi. There were times, said Marsan, that Warsidi spoke in bizarre terms. For example, on one occasion he said he wanted to have a child with horns and a tail. On another occasion, he began shouting at a crowded public gathering. For that reason, Ismed had a hard time believing that Warsidi had become a respected cleric in Cihideung. Ismed was also surprised to hear that many people wanted to come to Cihideung to learn the Koran from Warsidi.

At that point, some of Warsidi's visitors who had come to Cihideung to learn the Koran brought trouble. Several locals reported that their crops had been stolen. Their cassava was gone. Their bamboo was cut. Sometimes their coconuts were missing. The local community began to simmer. Ismed went to other surrounding communities, and they confirmed the thefts. Following that, Ismed gave a warning to his villagers to be careful with Warsidi.

Shortly thereafter, Warsidi became a bigger source of trouble for Pakuan Aji. Several witnesses saw Warsidi's followers wielding swords and learning how to use arrows. In addition, they were seen learning how to make bombs from empty bottles filled with gasoline, sawdust, and match powder. They began intensively training in martial arts, with headbands inscribed with slogans calling for jihad.

On occasion, Warsidi's followers became unruly. Many locals became uneasy, asking themselves why Warsidi and his group were stockpiling weapons. Ismed, moreover, could not understand how a worker like Warsidi could suddenly become a cleric—and then ask his disciples to make arrows and bombs in a tranquil place like Cihideung.

The answer to this mystery became obvious when Warsidi and his followers staged a riot, then shot poison arrows and cut the neck of the visiting military sub-district commander, Captain Soetiman. Soetiman's body was subsequently kept by them. This incident took many people by surprise and not only tainted the image of Lampung, but also left a bad impression on the international stage. The story of Captain Soetiman's murder is the climax to the mystery at Pakuan Aji.

Testimony from Mushonif and Fadhillah.

Warsidi was initially seen as a leader who could bridge the gaps among the opposing factions who supported the Indonesian Islamic State (*Negara Islam Indonesia*, or NII) concept. There had been much upheaval within the NII movement, even to the point of its members threatening and killed each other. Given this situation, Warsidi was seen as the only person capable of settling the dispute, even though he had never been a prominent personality in the NII movement. This is the view of Muhsonif, which was corroborated by the testimony of Fadillah.

Things began when a group from Ngruki, Central Java, lost their main leader, Abdullah Sungkar, who was forced to flee to Malaysia. When this took place, his followers fled to the sanctuary of an NII cell in Lampung. There, however, they found the movement's leaders—Muhammad Rifai and Zainal Arifin—locked in conflict over who would become the local chairman. Both saw themselves as the rightful NII chief in Lampung. At the same time, there was a small group in Jakarta that dreamed of building a Muslim commune, just as was being done in Malaysia. This Jakarta group included Sudarsono, Nurhidayat, and Achmad Fauzi.

These are the vying groups behind the Talangsari turmoil in Central Java. As they bickered over who would be their leader, the choice ultimately fell on Warsidi. Why did they chose Warsidi? According to Mushonif, it was because Warsidi had land in Cihideung. Though it was small—just 1.5 hectares—this was considered sufficient for their purposes. Moreover, Lampung was considered better than other places—like West Nusa Tenggara—because it was not too far from Jakarta.

At the time of the Cihideung unrest, Mushonif, 24, was not directly involved with Warsidi's activities. At the time, he was teaching with Usman at the Al Islam Labuhan Ratu boarding school, not far from Cihideung. While there, he saw Warsidi as a person who was properly struggling for the ideals of Islam. In his opinion, Warsidi was a suitable leader because he consistently spoke out and took action. Moreover, Mushonif was impressed with Warsidi's intention to build a religious commune (even though he later came to know that it was originally Darsono's idea).

Mushonif never imagined that his ties with Warsidi would land him ten years in jail in Nusakambangan. In court, this bespectacled man was seething with hate toward the authorities and New Order government, which he considered corrupt and unjust.

Unlike Mushonif, Fadillah from the start respected Warsidi. He felt that Warsidi felt more concern for others than himself. All through Warsidi's life, said Fadillah, he was dedicated to this struggle. Even in the last seconds before death, he said that it would be better to die with faith than surrender to an infidel.

This kind of commitment made Fadhillah unwavering in his view that Warsidi was his leader of choice. Warsidi's goodness was difficult to measure. For example, when Fadhillah had escaped to the jungle, it was only Anwar Warsidi that wanted to meet him. This touched Fadhillah's heart, like poetry illuminating the jungle.

Warsidi asked Fadhillah to join in his struggle. This struggle, he said, should not be performed alone. If there are any friends, he asked, why should they be left alone in the bush? These were the words uttered by Warsidi after he met Fadhillah in the jungle. Fadhillah was touched. Not long after, he moved with his family to join Warsidi and face the future.

In Cihideung, Fadhillah waited for a real leader to emerge. Not someone like Abdullah Sungkar, who left his followers and fled to Malaysia. And not leaders who appoint themselves as chief clerics, like Zainal Arifin or Muhammad Rifai. Although such a perfect leader had not emerged before the Talangsari incident, Fadhillah retains love and respect for Warsidi until now.

Warsidi, *Mbedagol*

The term *mbedagol* is not widely known among the public at large. However, it is commonly used by certain groups in Central Java. It refers to an egotist, a fanatic, someone who refuses to hear the opinion of others. This is the image given by Suryadi, 49, when telling his experiences with Warsidi over several years in Cihideung, Central Lampung.

Suryadi was from Solo, Central Java, and moved to Lampung with no intention of staying in Cihideung, much less meeting a person named Anwar Warsidi at Marsan's house in Hujan Mas village, Pakuan Aji. He had intended to stay a short time to work as a laborer at a pepper plantation.

As a member of the Abdullah Sungkar group from Ngruki, Central Java, he had escaped to Lampung because he was wanted by the Javanese authorities. He did not know much about Warsidi, and after their first meeting he emerged unimpressed. Still, he remained in contact until the time he was at Jayus's house in Cihideung. While Warsidi was in charge of maintaining Jayus's prayer room, he progressed plans (proposed by Darsono's group in Jakarta) to establish a religious commune.

According to Suryadi, he did not look upon Warsidi favorably because he always contradicted his stated principles. For example, he always quoted the Koran and the sayings of the Prophet, even at times when it was not appropriate for him to do so.

This controversial leader, for instance, would say that other persons are infidels. He opposed the government, criticized Pancasila, and permitted murder if it did not conform to his way of thinking. Suryadi describes Warsidi as an egotistical leader who found it difficult to accept other opinions. He always had a ready response to questions posed by others. For example, when he was criticized for his teachings on the Koran, he answered that those listening were not Arabs and therefore could not know the Koran if they could not fluently read it.

Because of this, Suryadi grew sour to living in Cihideung with Warsidi. One year before the uprising, he moved away.

Warsidi Eats Last

In the beginning, Arifin bin Karyan, 44, saw Warsidi as an ordinary man who did not have any great specialty. However, after a long period of living with Warsidi, he could not ignore this rare leader. Day after day, Arifin came to the Cihideung complex. After much depression, his heart became content after meeting Warsidi. In Talangsari III, he became full of life even though he ultimately lost his whole family.

Together with his wife, two children, and a cousin, Arifin departed from Tanjung Priok, Jakarta, and headed for Lampung. He intended to improve his standard of living, but he also was willing to use the opportunity to expand his religious study.

In Lampung, he was warmly welcomed by other Islamic followers who had come before him. He still fondly recalls the moment. At that time, Warsidi introduced himself as the group's leader. Arifin saw Warsidi as a simple man, full of concern and responsibility. Each morning, Warsidi's wife came to the followers and asked them whether they had enough provisions for the day, such as rice.

When having a meal, the children came first, then the mothers, then the fathers. Warsidi always had his meal last. Arifin bin Karyan had many months of such experiences living with Warsidi and his group.

There were many pros and cons concerning Warsidi. There were moments of sympathy, and moments of insult. Warsidi's life left an impression on many people, especially his loyal followers. He became a model opportunist. But only an opportunist who does not let his heart grow empty of the light of God will win. Other kinds of opportunists will be losers.***

SUKIDI

A.M. HENDROPRIYONO

K.H. MUH. ICHSAN

K.H. MARZUKI THOHIR

ACHMAD SARIKUN

SUDARSONO

FADHILLAH

5

LET HIM SPEAK

WHEN this book was being composed, there were recent media reports that the situation in Gunung Balak was not secure. Hunger and poverty had hit Central Lampung, making the community fearful of robberies and plundering. This is the same area where the Talangsari turmoil—the events in this book—took place. There were also reports that the local community did not want to speak to certain parties they suspected of exploiting the Talangsari incident, such as some of the NGOs that reportedly operated in the area.

The facts gathered in the field were far different from those portrayed in the media. The local community, in reality, was very cooperative and friendly. They told the truth about the earlier events surrounding Warsidi and Talangsari. From their testimony, one could detect sadness, as well as anger.

Warsidi's final performance came with many things that the local community could not understand. The mystery surrounding his life, which caused many problems for many people, is still a puzzle. And what appears in the mass media concerning Warsidi and Talangsari is, for the most part, untested much less proved.

The local community feels it has been cheated and deceived about Talangsari and Warsidi, as if they have been fed a line by a Javanese comedian. The community now intends to tell the truth about various incidents that took place 11 years ago. Let them speak!

Sukidi

❖ *The former head of the Talangsari III hamlet, he is an elder within the local community.*

Certainly, Sukidi did not imagine that his name would become known by many people and recorded in the country's national history. A farmer originally from Banyuwangi, East Java, he had been in Lampung since 1972. His only hope was to some day live on his own plot of land—something that was difficult if he remained in his hometown of Banyuwangi. A diligent worker, he was not dreaming. After almost 28 years in Lampung, he now had 1.5 hectares for his house and 1.5 hectares for his rice field and farmland.

Is he prosperous? Not yet. However, within his community he is respected. In fact, he was named hamlet chief for several decades. Today, he is a village elder.

He is a person to whom others come to confide their problems within the village.

During the timeframe in question, one member of the community complained to Sukidi that his cassava plants were being plundered by unknown persons. This was unusual, since everybody in the community already had their own cassava crop. Sukidi took it upon himself to investigate. It became apparent to him that a new community had taken shape—a community that had changed the village tradition to include taking other person's crops without permission. The behavior of this new community became an issue, not only within the community at large, but among the village authorities.

Because of this issue, it was feared that discontent among the locals could spread in an unpredictable fashion. In fact, from a trivial incident, it escalated into a major event causing the deaths of dozens, with their cries being echoed abroad. Even Sukidi, the ordinary citizen who came from a small village, had his moment in the spotlight.

This 48-year-old man has emerged as a primary and insightful source of information on Warsidi. He was the first official treated in a very improper manner by the mysterious cleric who incited the turmoil in Central Lampung.

How did you get to know Warsidi?

I first got to know Jayus, as he used to play volleyball with me when we were young. I came to know Warsidi after the RW [neighborhood watchgroup] head, Rasemin, told me that there was a guest at Jayus's house who had stayed a long time but did not report his presence. I told Rasemin that this guest had to report. Rasemin tried, but failed. I then met Jayus. With him were about five visitors that did not have identity cards. When I asked them about their origin and destination, they did not want to say anything. From Jayus, I was able to learn that one of the guests was named Mr. War. Several days later, there was news that Jayus was receiving more and more visitors, some of whom were acting strangely. Later, I found out that this was Warsidi and his group. This was on 15 December 1988.

How many were there by that time?

When I personally checked, there were only five persons that I did not know. I asked them to produce their identity cards so as not to cause any suspicions. They said they would, though they were just lying.

What was your first impression when you met Warsidi?

He was average, just an ordinary man. He did not exhibit anything strange or unusual. However, he was very closed. I heard that he had been to Pakuan Aji, the village next to mine. There he lived in Marsan's house and was a laborer in the pepper farm owned by Marsan. Warsidi was a migrant, and he later stayed at Cihideung. It turned out that Jayus allowed him to live on his land and gave him 1.5 hectares for his use. Together with his followers, Warsidi built a place that he could use as an Islamic study center. At this Islamic commune, the village community came to know that they were cursing and humiliating the government.

Was Jayus a rich man?

He was just an ordinary man like me. He was a village farmer. But he used to run a business making roof tiles and had a small building for prayers. In this place, Jayus and Warsidi used to perform their activities. I know Jayus well because both of us come from Java.

What was the name of his prayer building?

The people here called it Jayus's Mosque. It was built by Mr. Karma, his father. I know that whole family well, since they are long-term residents. After the arrival of Warsidi and his followers, the building was renamed Mujahidin Mosque.

How was the situation after Warsidi's arrival?

A lot of people complained, and there was unrest. The village community was not sympathetic to the attitude of the newcomers. Their words were strange to us—like calling the government infidels and saying Pancasila was illegal. They also considered that anybody who did not support them was an infidel. What really angered the community was when their crops were taken without permission. If we spoke to them about it, they immediately threatened us. I reported all this to Amir Puspa Mega, the village chief from Rajabasa Lama. I was asked by the village chief to heighten my vigilance. I established a neighborhood watch system along with other village officials. Following that, we received many reports that more people were coming to Jayus's house.

How long did this situation persist?

For almost two months, the community was stressed. Many of Warsidi's followers carried machetes and would swing them as they walked along the road. Locals also saw a place where they were shooting arrows and practicing martial arts. Finally, there were reports that they had collected empty bottles, which they said they were going to use to make bombs. As a result, the community got more worried, especially after they prohibited the locals from carrying flashlights or conducting the neighborhood watch at night. When they prohibited this, the community got more confused.

What did you do?

I went to their place, together with a non-commissioned officer who was posted in the village. It seemed like they objected to our arrival. They teased us by using foul language. One of them even went in front of the non-commissioned officer and farted. This is a fact. I was worried that the non-commissioned officer would get angry, and the situation would get very dangerous. Knowing that tension was rising, I immediately left. But when I was on the way out, I discovered that my motorbike was gone. I asked them about it, but they gave no reply. I turned on my flashlight to look for it, and I found that it had been thrown beside the Beringin River. I recovered it. Just after I took a couple of steps to start my motorbike, two of them held my arm and said, 'Mr. Kidi, if you come back again tomorrow, don't come with just two people.' They said this with such hate! I tried to get out of there as fast as I could. But they caught me. I was worried, and again I took off. I looked at my watch; it was 11 at night. After that I heard that some of Warsidi's followers were trying to hunt me down. My family escaped, and I did not go home since they took over my house.

Why didn't you report this to the police or other officials?

By the morning of Friday, 3 February, I reported to the village office. They forwarded my report to the district office. That night (Friday night), two persons came from the district office: a non-commissioned officer and a person from government affairs. They came to have a dialogue with Warsidi. The situation got critical. They were threatened by machetes and sickles by Warsidi's followers. They got worried and immediately fled. On Sunday, 5 February, a delegation from Way Jepara again came. Sergeant Major Dahlan and Corporal Rachman accompanied them. I, as well as the leaders from the neighborhood watch program, went along with them to monitor the location. At 11 at night, we went secretly. That night, there were ten of Warsidi's followers controlling the guard post. After watching them, we then caught them. We successfully arrested six of them with their swords, machetes, sickles, Molotov cocktails, and a sack of arrows. Because many people in the village requested the arrows, there were only 23 left as material evidence.

After that, how was the situation?

That night, after the arrest, the village community saw that several of Warsidi's followers left their commune. It looked like they were moving, because they brought along their utensils, sleeping mats, and other things. They went to Pancasila village. I could not tell how many, since it was dark. But it was clear that some of Warsidi's followers were leaving their location along with their belongings.

What day was that?

It was Monday, 6 February. I remember quite well. Just around noon, at about 10 o'clock, I was requested by Major Sinaga, the military district chief, to accompany his group and guide them to the location used by Mr. Warsidi. The chief of the military sub-district was on his motorbike at the head of the column. The chief of the military district drove in a jeep, followed by the others in a second jeep. The district chief rode behind my group. Before entering the location, Captain Soetiman was intercepted by Warsidi's band. He was showered by arrows from the bush and from the watchpost. It was horrible.

Some have said that Soetiman shot his gun before entering the location?

This is not true. I saw it by myself. I swear that it not true. Before Soetiman shot his gun, the arrows hit him. The chief of the military district, who was still in his jeep, ordered him to come back, but the situation had gotten out of control. Each of us tried to save ourselves. I remember that at that moment, Captain Soetiman got off his motorbike, and he was attacked by people screaming, 'God is great, God is great, you are an infidel...' I saw it myself. Even when I ran east, I found an officer hit by an arrow in the chest. I saw Sergeant Yatim groaning, and I immediately dragged him up on the car. By the time I was beside the chief of the military district, I heard him firing his gun in the air. The chief ordered us to retreat, but his jeep was unable to move because it was blocked. Eventually, the jeep was turned around and they were able to flee by crossing a cassava farm. That is all of my story. I stayed at the village office until the Talangsari clash was over.

Why did you hold out in the village office?

If I left, it would be very dangerous. They thought that all this was because of me. That is why they were hunting me down to kill me. To monitor the situation, I entrusted several members of the community to stay in touch with me. From their reports, I knew that by noon several other groups had left Warsidi's location. Men, women, children—they were all going. A total of around 70 or 80 people. While they were leaving, they said, 'We don't want to follow Warsidi anymore. We want to live. Why do Muslims kill? We don't want to be killed, we want to live.'

So it looked like they had moved?

That's right, it looked like all of their commune was moving. Previously, I thought that the Warsidi complex was empty, or at least only the top leaders were still holding out. The whole village community knew that the commune had left. They moved not only through Talangsari, but also through Pakuan Aji and Kelahang. Most of them must have left Warsidi's place.

After the incident became known around the world, several NGOs have accused the security officials of violating human rights. What is your opinion?

According to me, this is not fair. Actually, the opposite is true. Those who violated human rights were not the officials, but Warsidi and his followers. The one who was killed first was an official, Soetiman. He was legally an official. Soetiman's superiors then felt it was their responsibility. After hearing that their subordinate was killed and his body was being withheld, they immediately took action to get back the body. But they were prevented from doing so. In fact, they were attacked and a clash broke out. Who is wrong? I see it as wrong if they try to prosecute the officials. What about Private Budi Waluyo, Sergeant Sudargo, Segeant Arifin Sembiring, and Santoso Arifin, the village head that was cruelly killed in Gunung Balak? All of the village community will object and will certainly be able to provide testimony. Especially since they have been victims of Warsidi's cruelty. The community suffered a loss, and their suffering is still being felt to this day. Actually, the ones who have a right to prosecute this case are us, since we have suffered the loss and became the victim.

Can you give examples of the sacrifices enacted on the village community?

Until now, if anybody from Talangsari III tries to apply for a job, he or she is always asked about their involvement in the Warsidi case, and they always encounter difficulties. It hurts our feelings. Everybody in the Talangsari III community has been forced to become very defensive. It is very serious, because the entire community feels victimized. We might even try to offer counter claims. We are very prepared. All of the villagers are ready to offer their testimony if the situation gets more tense.

It seems like a number of NGOs are still trying to investigate the Talangsari III case.

It is their right. But in my opinion, they should not make any problems because the villagers are certain to get angry. You believe it? Our communities want to live in harmony, peace, and security. This is the hope and demand of the Talangsari III community.

Suryadi

❖ *He claims that he was loyal to Abdullah Sungkar. After having spent several years with Warsidi, he lost his sense of peace. As a result, he left Warsidi a year before the trouble with the government.*

Suryadi is a preacher who originally hails from Solo. Many things come easy to him. He is good at public speaking, good at smiling. He is graceful and active, as if he is chasing something that was lost. Although he is fast to talk, others cannot easily predict what is on his mind. Although this forty-nine year old is able to say no, his heart might say yes.

This is what distinguishes Suryadi from K.H. Abdullah Sungkar, who always says the truth and says it openly. If Abdullah Sungkar saw someone who acted like a tyrant, then that is the word he would use. This even included Soeharto when he ruled the country. K.H. Abdullah Sungkar was the pioneer of Islamic study at Ngukri village in Solo, Central Java. Suryadi used to be his disciple, even though he now denies it.

How did you join Abdullah Sungkar?

Previously, I was interested in being a disciple of Sungkar. After joining his Islamic study group, I thought it was good and I liked him, until it was disbanded. The substance of his teachings pertained to being consistent and disciplined in one's faith. Be unshaken in the destiny of God. This is something I got from the Islamic study group at Ngukri. Unfortunately, this Islamic study group no longer exists. Abdullah Sungkar feared that he was going to be imprisoned by the government, so he fled. There have been recent news reports that he is in Malaysia.

How did you get to be in Lampung?

After the study group was disbanded, I went to Khusnul's house in Jakarta, who was one of Abdullah Sungkar's disciples. I did not fit in, because their attitude was too extreme and it went against what I felt in my heart. I went back to Solo. Without getting sufficient rest, I was told that I was being tracked by the government. I immediately went to Semarang to Thoha's house. There I met Budiman. Together with him, I went to Lampung, to Hasan Tiro's house in Braja Dewa. The head of the village chief in Braja Dewa was Ibu Sakeh, a woman who was married to Roja'i. This Roja'I was a member of the Ajengan Masduki chapter of NII, who had taken an oath with the NII governor for Lampung named Zaenal Arifin. By that time, the head of Way Jepara was Warsidi.

Who is Hasan Tiro?

He was the NII community leader. There were many guests in his house, including some from Temanggung and some others from Central Java. After not being there long, I was asked to go to Dalhari Nurmanto's house in Karang Anyar in Labuhan Maringgai. While I was working on farmland there, I was asked to teach Islam to his children. But I was not there long. Hasan Tiro asked me to go to a place named Umbul Hujan Mas in 1986. When I was in Umbul Hujan Mas, I met Warsidi and his followers over the course of three months when I was picking peppers on Marsan's farmland.

How did you know about Warsidi?

He told me about himself. He was born to a farmer's family in Magelang, Central Java. His father was named Marto Pawiro. He had many brothers and sisters; he was the youngest of nine brothers and sisters. He moved to Lampung with his parents when he was a teen, as a migrant to Metro, Central Lampung. One day when he was in a mosque in Metro, he met a cleric who was engrossed in prayers. Warsidi was interested and wanted to be his disciple. This man who Warsidi modeled himself after was Anwaruddin, who was to become Warsidi's teacher. Since then, Warsidi followed his teacher everywhere. When his teacher died, Warsidi took over his position, even marrying the teacher's widow. He even changed his name to Anwar Warsidi to be able to inherit Anwaruddin's knowledge. Warsidi then moved from one place to another until he came to Umbul Hujan Mas and met me there.

How did Warsidi come to be in Cihideung?

The distance from Umbul Hujan Mas to Cihideung is not far. It is only a couple of minutes. Warsidi used to perform his Friday prayers in Mr. Jayus's mosque; Jayus originally came from Banyuwangi and was a long-time Lampung resident. They used to discuss things with each other. Not long after that, Jayus offered a place near the mosque for Warsidi. I followed him there and became Mr. Jayus's employee, helping him make roofs while still keeping my profession as a preacher.

What do you know about Warsidi's teachings?

Warsidi taught nothing, but in my opinion he was very dangerous. One day, he said to me the words 'Illaha Ilallah,' and said that this meant the same as 'God.' He said that one who does not believe in God is the same as being empty, the same as the Indonesian Community Party, while Ilallah is the same as acknowledging God completely. Thus, if we want to know God, one must be previously empty, or previously communist, then filled by God to be totally Muslim. You should first see yourself as communist, then you just become a Muslim: this is what Warsidi taught. If this is taught to someone who does not understand religion, it is dangerous. It is also flawed in parts.

Some have said that he was not in line with the government.

Actually, what made him not in line with the government was how he spoke. There were many things he told me when I associated with him. For example, he said that laws apart from Islamic law were for infidels. He said that to salute the flag was paganism, and to work together was heresy. He said that our government did not follow Islamic rule and was illegal. These opinions were not shared by me. In my heart, I felt it was not right for a man like Warsidi to say such things because his knowledge about religion was not that good. I then left him to go teach religion away from Cihideung at Sidoredjo, Gunung Terang, Karang Anyar, and Pancasila village until 1988.

Where did you go after that?

I went back to Dalhari Nurmanto's house in Karang Anyar, Labuhan Maringgai, Central Lampung after Benny, one of Warsidi's followers, slandered me. He said that I was unholy, that I did not perform my prayers, and that my faith was void. He said that it was illegal to follow an apostate like me. Then the areas where I had previously established grew close to Warsidi. I no longer followed their progress until the Cihideung unrest broke out in 1989.

What is your last impression of Warsidi?

In my opinion, he was a very stubborn person. One had to follow whatever he said. If you are willing to follow him, he will be very close. It is as if he is willing to sacrifice his life for those that follow him. But if you are not willing to follow him, he can do many bad things, like slander you, even kill you. This included me. If I tried to give my views, he always had a response. I even tried to quote verses of the Koran. He would say to me, 'You are Javanese, so use the Javanese language, not Arabic.' He also said, 'Since we are not Arabic, it is not bad if we recite the Koran in the wrong way.' This is what he said to me when I associated with him in Cihideung.

Marsudi

❖ *Marsudi is Warsidi's elder brother. He used to boast he was the one who cut Soetiman's neck until he was dead. Is this something to be proud of?*

It has been a long time since the Talangsari turmoil, and Marsudi is now 65 years old. With a pale complexion and a wrinkled face, he does not look as wild as the time when he killed Soetiman. There is a tear in the corner of his eye, as if he is hiding a long story. From his thin lips, he still talks much, and he is still very vocal about the past—about the government, religion, and about his brother Warsidi.

On the morning of Monday, 6 February 1989, the situation at Warsidi's house in Cihideung hamlet was in suspended animation after five of his men were arrested by community officials the previous night. Warsidi ordered his people to be on full alert in the event there were more arrests.

At about 11100 hours, Soetiman and his group approached their location. One of the Warsidi's people cried, 'God is great!' and then his companions set upon sub-district chief Soetiman with weapons.

Marsudi suspected that Soetiman would conduct further arrests. When one of Warsidi's men cried 'God is great,' Marsudi interpreted this as a signal to attack. Watching Soetiman stagger while holding his weapon,

Marsudi chased him and stabbed him in his shoulder. Soetiman was still able to run off. Again, Marsudi chased him and cruelly cut Soetiman in the back of the neck. Soetiman, a brave officer, fell down and died instantly.

Marsudi, alias Mr. Su, the son of Marto Pawiro, spoke of his actions before a court. During the court session, Marsudi gave the appearance of being innocent. To this writer, Warsidi's elder brother, who was charged with Article 110 (1), Paragraph 107, Article 1, and paragraph 55 of the Criminal Code, told his story openly and in full.

Is it true that you cut down Soetiman?

Yes, it is. I cut down Soetiman. I saw him hit by the arrows but still holding his weapon. At that moment, he did not fire his weapon. He wanted to run, then I chased him and swung my machete at his shoulder. He was still able to run, so I chased him. Again, I swung my machete at the back of his neck. He fell right down. Then my other friends set upon him.

Why did you kill Soetiman?

Should I let him fire his gun at us? My friends had been arrested since Sunday night. They had arrested five and they had not been released. Then he came along, and he might have been coming to arrest more, so I thought it was better for me to kill him. Especially with the situation growing uncertain and uncontrollable, I had no choice but to kill him.

After killing Soetiman, did you regret it?

No, I didn't. I have never regretted it since he was wrong. He attacked us. I just did it for self-defense. To act in self-defense is good. If I died, I would have died in faith. We were innocent since we were attacked and arrested. That is why I did not regret killing Soetiman.

Where was Warsidi at that moment?

At the mosque. He was always at the mosque praying for his followers until the very end. On that morning, when the security forces had surrounded the Islamic study center, I tried to move but was shot. I then ran off to the mosque. At the mosque, Warsidi saw the blood. He was angry. I still remember what he told me: 'My elder brother, what has happened to you? Now it is my turn in battle!' He hurried off. After that time I was separated from him and did not see him anymore. I lost consciousness in the mosque, and was later wrapped in a mat by military personnel and thrown into a car. When I woke up, I was in the hospital.

What is your last impression of Warsidi?

Many say that Warsidi's face is similar to mine. In my village, sometimes people got confused between the two of us. It is hard to tell which one of us was the older one, and which was the younger one. His superiority was in speaking. One will be drawn by his speaking ability. I have only found one man like him. Warsidi was very patient, the most patient of men. Actually, he was a good man.

But many said that he ostracized the government. How was that?

Actually, many people got it wrong. Warsidi said nothing wrong. He only intended to enforce religion based on the Koran and the words of the Prophet Muhammad. That's all. It was not that he deviated from anything. From the start, Mr. Anwaruddin liked that. Warsidi and I were Mr. Anwar's followers unlike any in the past. Therefore, when the judge asked me about Pancasila, I said, 'Pancasila is illegal because it is a human creation. To pay taxes is also illegal, since it is not regulated by Islam. Rather, Islam calls for its own alms.' Concerning the government, I said, 'Government employees are worse than thieves because thieves are only cruel to rich men. But the officials are cruel to all, including the poor.' When the judge offered me a public defendant, I said, 'God and the Prophet will be with me and defend me.' Eventually the judge said, 'I would not be sentenced too long, just with a life sentence.' I replied, 'For two life sentences, I am ready. That would not be too long for me.'

What do you want in your life?

After Warsidi was gone, I wanted to die. During that time, I should have died. It is better that I should have died, because I have nothing. It was different with Warsidi, since he carried great hope. He expected to be a leader. Unfortunately, he died first.

Are you still with your wife?

Today, no. I have been married twice. My first wife was named Fathonah, and she bore me three children: Chiril Anam, Ikhya, and Nurhidayat. Her parents arranged for our divorce because they did not like me pursuing Islamic studies, especially after they knew I joined with Anwaruddin. I was forced to divorce my wife even though we still loved each other. My second wife was named Juminah and we had four children. This was the Juminah that I brought to Cihideung with Warsidi. When the turmoil broke out, Juminah was killed along with two of my children, Subur and Surip.

What is the story of Kiai Anwaruddin, who you say was an Islamic teacher?

Actually, Kiai Anwaruddin was not just my teacher, but also Warsidi's teacher. We met in Batanghari Mosque in Metro, through my brother-in-law, Zainuddin. The reason was because Warsidi and I admired this cleric who had a broad view. Unfortunately, this cleric got into a conflict with the surrounding mosques, so we had to move from one place to another. Once year later, he died. Warsidi married his widow. Not long after that, Warsidi got into some problems with the community, and he moved to Kotabumi and I went back to Metro. Finally, Warsidi found a new place in Cihideung. Then I was with Warsidi when he built the commune, until the time when the incident took place.

What is your impression of Kiai Anwaruddin?

He was intelligent and brave. He said, 'Soekarno was a tyrant.' Then he was arrested in Metro in 1965. Before the court could sentence him, the G30S coup attempt broke out, and they failed to prosecute him and he was set free. After getting free, his followers did not want to acknowledge him anymore. They were in conflict, and eventually he moved from one place to another until getting to North Lampung.

What about his views of Soeharto?

Anwar had not yet met Soeharto. Later he died. Then my younger brother, Warsidi, replaced him. If Cleric Anwar said that Soekarno was a dictator, Warsidi said that Soeharto was a dictator. Both were dictators. And as bad people, their dictatorial governments should not be followed. That is why we were vocal against dictatorial governments. Then we were criticized. We were labeled as the government's enemy.

Where were you born?

I was born in Sebrang Rowo village, Borobudur sub-district, Magelang district, in Central Java. My father is Marto Pawiro, a farmer with nine children. I am the sixth and Warsidi is the youngest. The children were Marjudi, Maryuni, Marsandi, Marsiyah, Marsidi, Marsudi, Suwandi, Dul Bahri, and the last, Warsidi. My father brought us as migrants to Lampung; we followed Maryumi, my elder sister, who was already there. In Metro, we met Kiai Anwaruddin.

Now where do you live?

I live in Metro, with my mother-in-law, Ibu Yomi. I spent ten years in prison in Nusakambangan. I want to spend my old age in Batanghari, Metro, Central Lampung.

Achmad Sarikun

❖ *He was entrusted by Warsidi to build a base in Gedung Wani, Central Lampung.*

Gedung Wani village, about 25 kilometers from Talangsari III in Cihideung, was a base for Warsidi's struggle against the government. The plan failed because the freshly-built structures at Gedung Wani were made out of bamboo, and they were burned by mobs only a few days after the Cihideung incident took place.

Some say that the local community was suspicious of Sarikun, Warsidi's loyal follower, who displayed strange behavior. For example, some of his children were forced out of the state-run elementary school. Since that time, he believed the only truth was the teachings of Warsidi. The substance of Warsidi's teachings held that the present should be the same as the time of the Prophet Muhammad. He saw it as legal to conduct a struggle to bring this about. Later, it became known that Sarikun made an oath to Warsidi and volunteered part of his land to be used as a base camp for Warsidi's movement.

This camp was built on 1 hectare of land. The village community got angry, as they did not want their village to suffer the same fate as Talangsari III. On the morning of Saturday, 18 February 1989, they burned down the structures at the base.

Now 60 years old, Achmad Sarikun still spends his time at Gedung Wani after being released from Nusakambangan prison. The following is an interview with him.

How did you come to associate with Warsidi?

I heard from some people that there was a good Islamic teacher in Cihideung. I went there and saw it for myself, and became interested in following him. I acknowledge that my religious knowledge was very poor. That is why, after entering Warsidi's group, I fit right in.

What made you fit in?

First, it was like there was harmony within the same family. I also felt like I fit in with the way he gave explanations. I directly understood that this was Islam. Concerning the five principles, I understood that they must be strongly upheld and implemented. From this, I felt that I was a real Muslim.

What did you get from this Islamic study?

Only at that point was I able to learn about my faith. Actually, the time went by too fast. I was not supposed to be like that. The incident was a real disaster and a test for me.

Why did you chose to go to Warsidi, not to another place like a boarding school?

I wanted to learn about Islam, and I found it there. I thought that all studies of Islam were the same. Since

I regarded that as good, I asked my wife and family to go there. Then the incident broke out. If the turmoil did not take place, I might still be there.

Some say that you were the man entrusted by Warsidi to build the Gedung Wani base.

Actually, it should not be called a base. This was a term used by journalists. A structure was erected as a small mosque. My friends who came from Cihideung often stopped over there. They often came to the adjoining dormitory, where they came to meet me. Maybe they saw me as their elder; maybe that is why they wanted to see me. The way that we met made me fell happy and honored. They were strong in their practice and cared for one another. This behavior was not to be found outside of Warsidi's group.

Was Warsidi's Islamic teachings good?

I didn't find any bad things there. They taught about religion, isn't that good? Maybe later there was a conflict with the community, involving government officials, but I don't know about that. I only knew the good things. You know, I only wanted to study Islam.

Some say that the group was against Pancasila and the government.

I didn't concern myself with that, especially since I was not there too long. The situation actually felt a bit stressed. Previously, I think the situation was normal, but after many people came there started to be many problems. I didn't think that the situation would change. I think the incident was like an accident.

Can you talk about the situation at that time?

Because the military man was killed by Mr. Marsudi, the situation got tense through the afternoon. Then the situation grew uncontrollable during the night. The incident from dawn through noon is hard to explain because many officials came there. In particular, Warsidi's group became uncontrollable.

When the tense situation broke out, what did you experience?

It is the most tense experience in my life, especially since my child was killed. I was really broken over the incident.

Who do you blame, Warsidi or the government?

I think both of them. Nothing would have been destroyed if they had understood each other.

Why do you blame Warsidi?

His followers were uncontrollable. When the incident broke out, they should not have resisted but should have surrendered. Actually, the ones who are most in the wrong are the ones who did not want to surrender. I myself do not know why they did not want to surrender.

Did some of them resist?

I saw the Jakarta group resist and display strange behavior. They did not want to be ordered to go out of their homes. The order to surrender was directed against them. If they had followed this order, there would not have been many victims. You can see that I was saved, as was my wife. At that time, my wife was told by some in the Jakarta group not to go out of the house. Mr. Marsudi, who was shot and unconscious, is still alive.

Who ordered you not to go out of the house?

It was Alex, one of the members of the Jakarta group. I didn't know much about them. It is not clear who they were.

From Warsidi's group, was there anybody else who resisted besides Alex?

Actually, there were a lot of them. But the ones who resisted the most were from Jakarta, led by Alex. They gave the order to resist the authorities and not to surrender. Eventually, Alex was killed and also Usman, along with their families.

When you were arrested, were you tortured?

No, I was only kicked and ordered to squat, then sent to the military region command. By that time, if everybody had been willing to go out and follow orders, there would not have been an incident like the one that transpired.

What was the error of the authorities?

They fired their guns. It made the situation more tense. Maybe they were worried, which made them unreasonable and uncontrollable. This is only my opinion, which might not be true.

Was anybody shot?

Honestly, I don't know. I only heard gunfire. I don't know if anybody was shot because by that time, I was facing downward. I was collected and taken somewhere, but to where I not longer remember.

Do you know who burned the huts?

I really don't know, since the incident was very fast. The fire flashed through the huts very fast. Everything was in such a panic, it is not possible to remember who burned them down and who was shot.

Some say that Alex was the one that burned down the huts.

It might be, but by that time I could not see. Some said that Alex's legs were shot. And only Alex knew where the gasoline was stored for making the Molotov cocktails. Why would Alex burn the huts, where the members of the commune were still located? If true, what was the reason? It is not clear. I have no comment.

How many people were killed?

I don't know exactly. My son, Yusuf, was one of those killed, and so far I don't know where his grave is located.

How many houses were occupied by the Warsidi community?

I know of four houses, and one mosque. Each was occupied by between 15 and 25 people. There might have been a minimum of about 100 people all together.

From that total, were all killed?

Of course not. I am still alive. However, I don't know how many are still alive.

These days, officials are being blamed by certain interest groups. What is your comment?

In my opinion, I don't want to suspect or blame them since they were doing nothing more than performing their duty. Today there is reconciliation, so why continue to question this?

Who arranged for the reconciliation?

At that time, the authorities were represented by Hendropriyono, since he was the military region commander when the incident broke out. From Warsidi's side, he was represented by Darsono, me, and some others. I think that this was enough, since it complies with Islamic teaching. As far as I know, reconciliation is the most suitable solution.

Why?

Because Islam teaches that there should not be revenge. It is my opinion, I am not sure about the others. There is no perfect person. Those who were wrong should be reprimanded, and those who are wronged should forgive, that is all. That is my opinion.

Some have said that the reconciliation was due to money.

It is not true. If it was due to money, I certainly would not come because I am not willing to be bought. It is my opinion, I am not certain of the others.

Fadhillah

❖ *He had an important role when the Central Lampung incident broke out. He was the commander of Warsidi's force that caused the commotion in the southern part of Sumatra.*

When arrested, Fahdillah claimed that his name was Sugito. However, the Pakuan Aji community, who arrested him on 8 February 1989—the day after the Talangsari incident—was not easily deceived and saw through the ruse. The man born on 13 December 1959 in Tawangmangu Solo in Central Java finally admitted that he was Fadhillah,. Warsidi's commander who had caused chaos for an entire night in the capital of Lampung, moments before the Talangsari incident broke out.

Fadhillah has specific recollections when reminded of the incident. This man with strong convictions admits that he is very respectful toward Warsidi because Warsidi gave him much help when he was a fugitive from Central Java. Fadhillah at that time was one of the persons wanted by the authorities. He was one of the fanatic followers of Abdullah Sungkar, the Ngukri boarding school leader from Solo who had fled to Malaysia.

Abdullah Sungkar, who the government claimed was a fundamentalist leader, was very vocal against anything he saw in violation of the Koran. For Sungkar, the truth must not be hidden, but must be spoken openly. At the same time, that which is wrong should be exposed. For him, then, there was no problem saying that the government was full of infidels and its constitution was impure. Such opinions strongly influenced Fadhillah.

How could you come to be a fanatical supporter of Abdullah Sungkar's principles?

In 1985 in Solo, there was a place for Islamic study named Usroh. I joined this place. The longer I spent, the more interested I became. I eventually became very sympathetic until now, especially toward the teacher, Abdullah Sungkar. I was interested in him because he was the only one who was the most appropriate as a model religious leader. He had sophisticated knowledge, was polite and generous to all, was honest, and was not a hypocrite like some of the other clerics. The government hated him, actually. This might have been because of his frequent criticism and his statements that the New Order government was illegal because it was not run according to the Koran. Mr. Sungkar was going to be arrested, but he successfully fled to Malaysia.

How did you get to Lampung?

When they failed to arrest Sungkar, the government got angry. The Islamic study group was broken up. All of his followers were pursued, including me. It was better for me and my family to escape to Lampung, where many of my friends lived. I lived in Dalhari Nurmanto's house in Karang Anyar, Labuhan Maringgai, East Lampung, until the Islamic study group there was broken up. The leadership in Karang Anyar had been divided in two: Mochamad Rifai had one group, and Zainal Arifin had the other. Before it was broken up between these two people, Abdul Kodir Barozak had led the NII Islamic study group in Lampung. After he was imprisoned, this group was taken over by Zainal Arifin. However, Dalhari Nurmanto complained when his name was not listed among the community leaders. Dalhari got angry, so he promoted Mochamad Rifai as a new leader. With two leaders, the community got confused—including Warsidi, who was Zainal Arifin's subordinate. Warsidi left, choosing not to follow either leader. I lived in Dalhari Nurmanto's house, and was asked to kill Zainal Arifin, because it was feared that Zainal would kill Dalhari. I refused to do this, because Islam prohibits the murder of other Muslims. I decided not to join either of the two parties that were in conflict.

In other words, you moved into the forest?

I was temporarily separated from the community. I made firewood for survival. While I was in this desperate condition, Warsidi came to me and asked me to join his community. He said, 'If you still have friends, why do you live in the forest? Let us assemble and await a leader.' I went there and joined his group.

What do you know about Warsidi?

He was a good man and a good candidate as a leader. During that time, he asked Zainal Arifin to appoint him as the NII district head for Lampung. This took place in Cihideung, where Warsidi built his commune with people that came from various places in Java, including Ngruki and Jakarta.

What was Warsidi doing at that time?

He built a site, changing it from an ordinary house into a place to stage events. He asked for the counsel of Zainal Arifin and Mochamad Rifai, and neither offered any objections. So he then decided to invite Abdullah Sungkar from Malaysia to Lampung. Unfortunately, before he came the turmoil broke out. Eventually, Zainal Arifin was arrested, not just because he was a follower of Warsidi but also because he was involved with the NII. The fate of Rifai is still unknown.

What was the extent of Warsidi's relationship with NII?

Actually, we were an NII community. However, we no longer referred to it as 'NII' because by that time Warsidi's community had assimilated many groups from many backgrounds. For us, the most important thing was to prepare an Islamic commune; after that, we could become guerrillas.

For how long did you follow Warsidi?

Actually not too long. I met him since the time he was in Labuhan Maringgai. Then we met in Cihideung to build the Islamic center on the 1.5 hectares of land granted by Mr. Jayus. In addition, I also had the duty to help Mr. Sarikun to build a small mosque in Gedung Wani. The local community later burned down the small mosque in Gedung Wani.

How could you monitor events in Cihideung while you were in Gedung Wani?

I moved back and forth between Cihideung and Gedung Wani and kept in touch with several important persons. For example, I spoke with Mrs. Sakeh, the village leader of Brajadewa. Her husband, Rojai, was a member of Warsidi's community. He was a long-time NII activist. From the district office, Mrs. Sakeh got information that the authorities would raid Warsidi's place. This information was sent to Cihideung and Warsidi immediately placed his community on alert. His followers had to man their watch posts. The village community was prohibited to approach these posts. Not long after that, on 5 February, five of Warsidi's followers were arrested by the authorities. Warsidi got angry. That night, I was ordered to gain their release as best I could. However, before I could find the five, there was an outbreak of violence that noon. Captain Soetiman was killed and the situation at the commune got tense.

How did you look for the five followers who were arrested?

That night, I went with twelve friends on foot for several kilometers. We were carrying all kinds of equipment, like machetes, swords, arrows, and Molotov cocktails. At 0600, we had just reached the Way Jepara sub-district command. Before we entered the military sub-district post, we saw lots of people milling around. From them, we learned that the arrested persons had been moved to the military region command. We immediately departed for the military region command in Tanjung Karang.

If the arrested persons were still at the military sub-district post, what would you have done?

I planned to release them peacefully if possible. If not, I would forcefully release them. One way or the other, they were going to get released. But since they were not there, we decided to look for them in the city. Before we went to the military region command, we agreed to stop at Mr. Zamzuri's house in Sidoredjo to plan our strategy. Around 2:00 that afternoon, before we left, Beny and Sholeh came from

Cihideung. From them, we learned that there had been a clash at the commune. I headed to for the commune and reached there by 4:00. The situation was very tense, and Soetiman's body was being buried. In a meeting with Warsidi, he decided not to worry about the five arrested members anymore. Instead, our strategy was now to attack military outposts. In principle, we were supposed to make uprisings all over Lampung in order to take the focus off of Cihideung. Since we had killed a member of the security forces, we assumed that the authorities would automatically seek revenge against the commune. That is why we needed to stage terrorist attacks across Lampung.

What was your strategy to terrorize Lampung?

From Cihideung I went back to Sidoredjo to meet 11 of our troops. While there, we agreed to strike at the military region command and release our five friends who were being held there. Because the distance between Sidoredjo and the military region command was quite far, we decided to rent a car from Sribawono to Panjang. In the car, there was a member of the armed forces, Private Budi Waluyo, who was a passenger. When we rented the car, he did not want to get off there and intended to accompany us for the ride. While we were driving, we introduced ourselves. I asked him if he knew about the incident at Cidiheung. He said that he knew about the incident, and had actually taken part in it. Because of this, I killed him right away. The driver got scared and ran off with his assistant, leaving us in the car.

How did you kill him?

My friends held the man from behind. Then I stabbed him in his stomach and chest until he died. His body was left near an oil palm plantation in Wrekan. Because the driver ran away, my friend drove. After we reached Tanjung Karang, he complained that the steering was giving him trouble. When a policeman stopped near us, I raised my machete as if I were going to strike him. The police office got worried and stepped back. We continued our trip and got to the office for the *Lampung Pos* newspaper. I threw a Molotov cocktail, but it did not burn it down.

Why did you go to the Lampung Pos? What was the connection with your other mission?

Actually, there was no connection. But this newspaper had been printing a lot of falsehoods. We decided to bomb it so that it wouldn't publish any more lies. Fortunately, the Molotov cocktail did not work. We continued our trip, but the driver complained about the steering and was not able to continue any more. Finally, we left the car in the area of Tigeneneng, between Natar and Metro. We dispersed from there. I walked by foot to go back to the commune. I reached Cihideung at about 8:00 on Tuesday night. The commune had already been destroyed.

How could you enter? By that time Cihideung was closed off and strictly guarded.

That night, I did not know anybody was guarding that location. I only found out later. After I was arrested and I reached the military region command, one of the soldiers said, 'So you are the man that came that night? I saw you, but didn't want to shoot.' The night that I went there, it was raining hard, and it was very dark. The water in the river that we used for bathing was at flood stage. When I got tired, I slept in one of the burned-out houses. Actually, I knew about the Cihideung situation from the family of Mr. Sarikun when I stopped at Gedung Wani before entering Cihideung. However, I wanted to see for myself. At around 5:00 in the morning, I woke up and followed the river toward Pakuan Aji. I intended to go to Jakarta. When I reached Pakuan Aji, some of the locals arrested me, then I was overwhelmed by them and turned over to the authorities.

When you were in the military region command, did you meet Hendropriyono?

Yes, I did. I still remember it. While I was imprisoned, I was forbidden from going out, even to the toilet. Finally, I defecated in the jail cell. At that time, Mr. Hendro was passing by and he turned toward me. He probably smelled my feces. 'Did you defecate here?' he asked. I said, 'Where should I defecate? The door was locked.' He then scolded the guard and told him to clean up the floor. After that, I was ordered to come to his office. He asked me many things, as if I was his guest. He was very friendly.

Has Hendro ever beaten you?

Never. He told his subordinates that our group had a belief that we were sacrificing in the way intended by God. He told them not to hit us unless there was a good reason. After that, I was moved to Rajabasa for two months. Then I was sent to Nusakambangan until I was released.

Sudarsono

❖ *Sudarsono admits to being the person who made the poisoned arrows for Warsidi's group in 1989. He was also a leader of the Mujahiddin Fisabilillah Group, which provided the inspiration for the Islamic commune in Lampung.*

Darsono has several distinguishing features, including a discolored mark on his forehead which he got from prostrating himself during daily prayers. He speaks frankly, and does not pay lip service to anyone or anything. His eyes are full of question, and he is naturally suspicious of others. Born in Deli, Sumatra, on 21 April 1963 of ethnic Javanese parents, he says that he would rather die than see Islam not enforced as law.

His statements reflect his concerns about the progress of Islam in Indonesia. From these concerns sprang his idea to establish an Islamic commune in Cihideung, Talangsari III, Central Lampung. His idea failed not only for himself, but also for thousands of others—for how long, we don't know.

Darsono had one other concept: he was the originator of the poisoned arrows. His friends say that only Darsono was able to create the arrows used at Cihideung. They had a specific, unique shape. It was made from simple materials. He used old spokes from a cyclo fashioned in a shape similar to an arrow. If cyclo spokes were not available, he used small pieces of bamboo as a substitute.

It is almost certain that this energetic man did not think his ideas would cause so much hurt to so many people. But in fact, not everybody's efforts result in benefits; Mr. Darsono is a prime example.

From the beginning, why did you want to build an Islamic commune at Talangsari?

As a Muslim, I had a lot of concerns about the progress of Islam. During one of my Islamic study sessions with Nurhidayat, his ideas and opinions were in line with mine. Also in this study group, I met Usman from Usroh Ngruki, the Islamic study group from Solo. Usman was disillusioned because his teacher, Abdullah Sungkar, had fled to Malaysia and left his students behind. The Ngukri study group had been broken up, and its members chased by the authorities. Those who escaped moved to Lampung to follow Warsidi and to hold study session just like in Ngukri. When Nurhidayat and I intended to build an Islamic commune, Usman suggested two locations: Lampung or West Nusa Tenggara. I chose Lampung because not only was it closer to Jakarta, but there was a large Javanese community already there.

Where did you meet Usman?

He was in the study group of Abu Sulaiman Mahmud, a cleric under Daud Beureueh, who was considered a high teacher of Islamic teachings. Both Abu Sulaiman Mahmud and Abdullah Sungkar had similar ideas on the creation of an Islamic state. It was there that I met Usman. He was interested in my idea to build an Islamic commune. In order to realize this, I held a meeting at the Cibinong area of Bogor. Usman brought a total of five delegates from Lampung. From them, a leadership board from selected. The board was to choose a leader for the trip. I chose Usman, and the others chose Nurhidayat. Nurhidayat won by a vote of four to one and was chosen to lead the trip. When this was officially decided, they decided on who should go to Lampung. The decision was for Nurhidayat, Faze and myself.

Did Fauzi join you?

The embryo of the Lampung commune started from four contingents named Abu Bakar, Umar, Usman, and Ali. There was a leader for each contingent. Haris Amir Fallah led the Abu Bakar contingent, Arifin Agule led the Usman contingent, I led the Umar contingent, and Nurhidayat led the Ali contingent. The idea for this was copied from Darul Arqam in Malaysia. As it turned out, the contingent system was not well integrated and it broke up. The only ones left were Nurhidayat and I. Then we met Fauzi and Wahiddin in Condet, the place where followers of Abdullah Sungkar were studying Islam. Fauzi and Wahiddin planned to take over the two empty slots. But before this could happen, the Lampung incident took place.

How much did you and Fauzi know about the Lampung location?

I have been there three times, and Fauzi was there once. I asked him to go there. That is why Fauzi didn't know too much about the Lampung situation and its progress. When I inspected the location, I went on foot from Sidoredjo to Cihideung through Gunung Balak. In Cihideung, there was about 1.5 hectares of land planned for the commune, while Sidoredjo and Gedung Wani were planned as transit posts. The affairs in Lampung were fully controlled by Warsidi, while Nurhidayat controlled things in Jakarta. Fauzi did not know much about Lampung. That is why he later said that he was imprisoned because of me. If he frequently spoke about the Lampung case, it is only because he read the newspapers. He did not have much firsthand information.

When was the last time you went to Lampung?

Several days before the incident, one of the people from the Lampung commune came to Jakarta and reported that the Way Jepara sub-district chief had summoned Warsidi. However, Warsidi replied that the best government is one that comes from the clerics, and the worst clerics are the ones that go to the government. Nurhidayat and I went to Lampung to find out about the situation. In the meeting, it was agreed that Warsidi would fulfill the summons of the sub-district chief. The plan was that if the commune was broken up, the members would go back to their respective places of origin. However, when I turned back toward Jakarta, Warsidi's plan changed. They reverted back to their idea of resisting the summons. Some have said that after the sub-district chief failed in his effort to call Warsidi, he turned the case over to the sub-district military chief. It was after the intervention of the sub-district military chief that the Cihideung unrest broke out. The sub-district military commander was killed and his body was not turned over. That afternoon, Sofyan went to inform us that there was an incident at Cihideung. I was planning to go to Lampung, but was prevented by Nurhidayat. After that, we had no more communication with them.

Where did you go after that?

I escaped and was arrested six months later. While I was in prison, I was tortured for four months. I really experienced the violence of the Suharto authorities. Again and again I was given drugs. Toward the end, I was tortured with electricity. After four months of torture, I was sentenced to death, then reduced to a life sentence, then finally to a sentence of 17 years. In fact, I only spent 9 years in prison. After being rehabilitated, I was released and can now enjoy freedom.

It is said that you and some of your friends were involved in reconciliation. What is that?

Reconciliation in this case is a peace agreement to release my friends imprisoned at Nusakambangan. It was a proposal of Hendropriyono sent to the president. It was classified as a clemency proposal for Husein Al-Hasby (jailed for the Borobudur case), Sudiyanto (the Komando Jihad case), Afwan (the Kilat boarding school case), and Marsudi (Warsidi's older brother). All were released, thank God. This reconciliation took place after the victims of the Talangsari case (both from Warsidi's side and the armed forces) met with Hendropriyono. The conclusion of the meeting was that Hendropriyono would help the clemency application for the persons imprisoned in the Lampung case.

In another decision, Hendro provided employment in the form of shrimp ponds in Lampung for 32 persons, including 28 persons in Bima. By this process of reconciliation, all victims and their families have settled their problems and made a peaceful reconciliation in the Muslim way.

However, some have questioned the reconciliation, like Nurhidayat. What is your comment?

I am sorry about Nurhidayat's attitude, since it causes tension and causes shame. He claims that his friends are being exploitative, yet it is Nurhidayat himself that has made the most money by exploiting the Lampung case. This friction has been exploited by some NGOs for their own interests. For example, the Smalam Committee led by Fikri Yasin and the NGO led by Yopi Lasut have sowed confusion about the Lampung case with a lot of vigor. Those who benefit from this are the communists, those in East Timor, Irian Jaya, the PRD and those kinds of groups.

K.H. Muhammad Ichsan

❖ *He was the leader of the Roudhatul Hidayat boarding school in Mengadurng Sari village, Jabung sub-district, Central Lampung.*

This boarding school was not under the influence of Warsidi. Warsidi's influence was felt among many of the Islamic schools in a 30-kilometer radius.

At that time, Muchammad Ichsan was uneasy because Warsidi had sent his members to stop the rituals normally conducted in the Roudhatul Hidayat school. For example, they asked him to stop the rituals of *tahlilan* [a series of prayers following a funeral] and *mauludan*. Warsidi said it was because Islam did not recognize such rituals, and that the activities at the Roudhatul Hidayat school were considered nonsense.

Of course, this made Muchammad Ichsan, who is a cleric within the NU Islamic movement, greatly annoyed. Ever since he began studying, he never heard anybody prohibiting the practice of *tahlilan*, let alone calling it impure. Indeed, if *tahlil* is translated as a series of prayers, then it is not only advocated by the Prophet, but is an order from God.

What was your reaction at the time?

I did not agree and many people were upset. Fortunately, he went away and did not come back anymore. Otherwise, I don't know what would have happened.

What do you know about Warsidi?

I heard about many issues. For example, he took the crops of others without feeling guilty. He said that anybody outside his group were infidels, even including clerics, if they did not support him. He was against the government and made weapons for war such as Molotov cocktails, swords, and poisoned arrows. There were several other issues that caused anxiety among the people. At first, I did not believe it. But after some of his people visited here and prohibited *tahlilan*, I believed it.

Was there anybody within your community that was a victim of Warsidi?

Yes. One person had his motorcycle taken. Initially, he had stopped because he had seen a commotion. As he approached, he was stabbed.

Was he dead?

No. He was able to escape. But his motorcycle was seized by that group and taken to the jungle. You see, Warsidi's group was not just in Talangsari, but all the way to Sidoredjo. They conducted unrest there. One week later, the locals in that area found the missing motorcycle in the forest. The person who had lost the motorcycle was accused of being one of Warsidi's followers. He was arrested, and they took him away. His name was Husni, and he was one of the NU people in this area.

What were the typical characteristics of those in Warsidi's group?

If another person did not want to join them, they were said to be infidels and their blood was impure. This is very dangerous. Many eyewitnesses spoke about the behavior of Warsidi's movement. There was even a joke that is somebody entered that commune, they would become crazy. He took the crops from other people without permission. The children who went to school were asked to quit by their parents. It later became apparent that the Warsidi movement had some followers in Gedung Wani not far from here, because some persons from here also participated. In the end, they even killed Captain Soetiman, the head of the military sub-district in Way Jepara.

Why did they conduct this murder?

They considered it legal to kill officials because the authorities were infidels. So when they were summoned by the military sub-district chief, they were not willing to go and said that clerics should not go to government officials. It was Warsidi's reasoning that led them to kill somebody. They had prepared themselves by making bows and arrows, Molotov cocktails, and so on, and even practiced martial arts.

How did you come to this area?

In the past, there were many illegal activities here, like gambling, stealing, robbing, and so on. The stealing in this area made it unsafe, and the gambling was uncontrolled. They bet on cockfights from the time they were children until adults. Their way of speaking was very bad. I felt very sad. If such activities continued, it would damage future generations. Finally, I came hear to teach the Koran to children. In the beginning, there were only one or two students. Later, there were many that wanted to study.

After that?

I established a group for women who wanted to study the Koran. In the beginning, there were only three women, but then the number increased. After four years, there was a good turnout. The community was getting better. Their religious activities were running smoothly, up until the time the Warsidi group showed up.

What did the Warsidi group do at that time?

First, they joined in the activity of teaching the Koran. In the course of that, they conducted questions and answers. Then they held debates, but the people became confused and uneasy. Moreover, they prohibited certain

Muslim practices. He said that these were not authorized. Those who prayed for the dead, for example, were said to have lost their way. In principle, they offered many opinions, and they began to go against what I had said.

According to you, what were they like?

It was clear that they would not be accepted by the community and they would cause social conflict. This proved the case, as a revolt finally broke out and they made trouble for many people. First, they wanted to teach here. But it could not be done because they were conflicts.

What else did they say?

They asked the community to follow Warsidi's group because they said it was time for them to follow Islam in a pure and correct manner. They said that those who do not want to join meant that they did not want to uphold Islam. Such persons are not Muslims and are infidels. Infidels always carry out actions prohibited by Islam. They said that respecting anybody other than God was the act of an infidel. This included saluting the flag. They said that anybody saluting the flag was questionable.

What is your opinion about Warsidi and his group being banished?

Those of us from the boarding school thanked the authorities for their prompt action. If not, we would have been forced to take action ourselves. If we had been forced to do so, there might have been more victims. If the authorities did not restrain us, we would have taken action and there would have been a huge conflict.

These days, some NGOs have leveled charges against the authorities. What is your opinion?

We are of course not happy about this. Why are they blaming the authorities? If this happens, we will defend them because it is clear that Warsidi's group was the one that made trouble for the local people. In fact, the authorities should be commended, not criticized.

What kind of defense would you offer?

Whatever they want, we will respond. In principle, both physically and spiritually, we can not accept the premise that the authorities are considered guilty for stamping out Warsidi. We do not agree with this because it is not appropriate to call the party that acted on behalf of many people to be guilty. I think the people who make such charges are guilty of making turmoil in Lampung.

Do you know of other parties that want to blame the authorities?

I have read items in the newspapers. I am saddened when I read this. I am ready to be a witness if necessary. I have checked in the local area, and the people of Lampung, especially around Talangsari and the boarding school, are ready to defend the authorities. We are ready to give evidence that Warsidi was the instigator in creating trouble for the people, and for staging a revolt.

What is your comment to the NGOs?

If they want to reopen the case, please do so. But please say the truth. Don't deceive the people by spreading lies. Please recheck the facts and ask the community about their opinion. There was an armed conflict, and they should know the rules about such conflicts.

What does Islam say about the rules of conflict?

War will occur if one party attacks the other. Those that pass away in the field of battle will be called the casualties of war. But don't make war with those who do not want to fight. War against crime is permitted. There is a saying, which means that the truth will prevail and the devil will lose.

K.H. Marzuki Thohir

❖ *The leader of the Miftakhul Hudd and Miftakhul Fallah boarding schools in Way Jepara, East Lampung, he is a member of the DPRA in East Lampung.*

Kiai Marzuki Thohir, 60, had unique insights into the controversial Warsidi. Now entrusted by the local community to represent them in the East Lampung regional assembly, he was greatly saddened when Warsidi called him an infidel because he held different views from the Cihideung commune leader.

Thohir, who now runs two boarding schools, recalls those earlier events like they were yesterday. He still remembers walking in front of some children in 1989, and then hearing them say they were going to make bows and arrows to kill infidels.

Kiai Marzuki comes across as a cleric who is diligent and clever in his speech. His smile is reflected not only in his lips, but also in his eyes.

When he was visited in his house—which is five kilometers from Warsidi's old location—Kiai Marzuki's face shows hints of his past memories.

Can you explain what took place?

At the time, I had many people who were in my Koran study group. This included people in the

Cihideung area in Talangsari, and also included people who were in Jayus's small mosque. But my activities, which were well run by the community, came under criticism. Those members that differed with Warsidi's group were said to be infidels. That included me, because I had initiated these activities before Warsidi arrived.

What else do you know about Warsidi?

In general, the entire community was not considered suitable by him. It was like oil and water. Warsidi's group was the exact opposite of the government. They called their location 'Al Mahdil Aqwal,' which means 'a place to mobilize power.' They declared the property of infidels to be impure, and therefore they were permitted to seize things from those properties without paying.

Did they train for war?

Yes, indeed. Even before the Talangsari turmoil, I saw many children making arrows. They said, 'Let's go make arrows to kill the infidels.' I was passing by at the time when they said it.

So the children sang a song like that?

At the time, I was really tense. The children did not understand the issues, but had been taught to hate and kill. The locals also did not understand why those in the commune were making arrows and why they were being called infidels. This is what really occurred at Al Mahdil Aqwal. Thank God that the authorities immediately took action.

But why are the authorities being accused and blamed?

I do not know, but the truth will prevail. There is no doubt about that. To make such claims without a basis is a crime. We will defend the truth. Moreover, the Talangsari problem is a problem of the people. Let the people speak and defend them. Those who accuse the authorities are uncontrolled. There are other interests involved that do not want to uphold justice and the truth. They just use university students to get money for their own interests. If they continue, they will have to face the locals and the boarding school community.

There are claims that certain parties will visit Warsidi's former location. What is your opinion?

If their agenda is to reopen the old conflict again, we will oppose it. If would be better if they do not conduct such an agenda because it has no usefulness for the people. It would be better to finish the mosque that is now being built there. The community will be happy because they are now tired of the Warsidi incident. Don't burden them further with such difficult issues. The Talangsari people and those in the surrounding areas will be upset.

Concerning Al Mahdil Aqwal, did the community know about it?

It was know, actually. I had actually raised it. I said that Al Mahdil Aqwal at Cihideung is a kind of revolt against the government through a religious institution. It will fall apart and will inflict suffering on us. This is what happened, because the government then assumed that boarding schools are always the center of revolts and cause riots.

What were the characteristics of this commune?

If they used the Koran, they only used an incomplete verse out of context and they magnified it as the truth of Islam. The same was true about how they used the precepts of the Prophet. Sometimes, they spoke of jihad. All people are infidels, they said, except for their group.

What were the differences between Al Mahdil Aqwal and a boarding school?

Boarding schools are clearly the centers of study for students looking to enrich their knowledge of Islam. Al Mahdil Aqwal, by contrast, was used as a place to assemble power for a revolt. Therefore, they made bombs, bows and arrows, as well as meditated and pursued other kinds of knowledge.

After Warsidi and his gang were banished, what became of the local community?

The community really thanked the government authorities that were successful in putting an end to

Warsidi's activities that had gone against the people. Warsidi frequently said that the community was not run in accordance with the Koran and the sayings of the Prophet. I relayed this to the head of the military region command in Lampung, and said that this was because of their incomplete understanding of the Koran and the sayings of the Prophet. If left unchecked, it would be easy for the people to start accusing others of being infidels. This could endanger the development of Islamic life.

What about the government authorities and clerics, who came under question by Warsidi?

He was like a small child in his understanding of religion. The true meaning is not so simple. We must look at the purpose and context of the religious writings. We must not talk nonsense. From the past, such issues have long been discussed. If Muslims view such issues in his manner, we will have no progress.

How long were you in contact with Warsidi and his group?

Before Warsidi came, my activities had reached Cihideung without any trouble. Then they came and joined with us. When I explained about some teachings, they protested and said my activities strayed from Islamic law. According to them, there was an obligation to pray together. I said that there was an obligation to pray, but not necessarily to pray together. Since that time, we took our separate ways.

After this incident, what was your reaction?

I explained myself to my people, who held the same opinion as me. I said that those who agreed should stay, and those who disagreed should leave. In the end, we parted ways. I told them that this was dangerous. This was proven when they established Al Mahdil Aqwal.

How many persons were there at that time?

When I was still there, there were between 15 and 20 persons. I am not exactly sure after all this time. Maybe it was more.

How about those who say there were hundreds at the commune?

Clearly they are lying. No matter how you measure it, the commune could not accommodate hundreds of people. Nobody can believe that.

When you first met Warsidi, what was your opinion of him? Did he possess any special characteristics of a cleric?

As far as I was concerned, his religious knowledge was very limited, especially about the Koran and how to read it. According to me, he was a reckless person.

Now, many NGOs are trying to reopen the Talangsari case. What is your opinion of this?

If they want recognition from the community, they must tell the truth. They cannot say something is right if they know it is wrong. I think that those persons who claim to be working on behalf of NGOs are of low quality. That is why they frequently drift outside of logic and certainty.

There are some that say Warsidi's group should be defended because they were treated unjustly. What is your opinion?

If those who say this are in Lampung city or in Jakarta, they should be ignored. They generally do not know about the issue. They are just seeking to profit from it. When they say they are speaking on behalf of an NGO, then they can get money easily.

What is your message?

Once again I say that Warsidi and his group did not act in harmony with the local community. They were like oil and water. Their presence was not wanted. Besides hurting the community, they threatened and intimidated the people. They also acted dishonestly. They claimed that they had a business dealing with roof tiles, but after they were paid they did not deliver the tiles. I am one of the persons that they cheated.

A.M. Hendropriyono

❖ *The former commander of* Black Garuda *Military Region 043 in Lampung is now getting into trouble. Some opportunists have taken a dislike to him. But all the locals, down to the hamlet level, support him.*

Some may be upset, and they may not want to believe the truth. But the following is the true story of Hendropriyono. He ventured to the far end of the Talangsari hamlet looking for his subordinate who was murdered by Warsidi. He could have chosen to remain like a bird in a cage, merely watching the time go by. When there was an emergency situation, he could have fled, coming back only when the situation got better. This would have been the safe path. He would not have had as much responsibility, and he could have claimed he was not involved.

Now things have become uncomfortable for Hendro. Eleven years after the Lampung incident, there are opportunists that want to take advantage of him. Achmad Fauzi bin Isnan, for example. This is a person who had been close to Sudarsono, but did not have much first-hand knowledge of Lampung. But he has spoken a lot about Lampung recently, and has tried to benefit at Hendro's expense. When he was once questioned about his current activities, Fauzi smiled and said that his current project is to stomp on Hendro's foot.

If this is the case, Fauzi's project has been a success. The community has started to formulate opinions after Fauzi supposedly unearthed sins of Hendro and conveyed them to the press. Though Fauzi might be happy because he feels he has succeeded in stepping on Hendro's toes, this book recounts the true details in the following chapter on A.M. Hendropriyono.

In this chapter, the author initially wanted to conduct an interview with A.M. Hendropriyono about the Lampung incident. But the author found that the written text he received closely matched what he had found in his field research. The author then decided to print the text in its entirely in order to convey the full contents directly to the community on the issues that directly effected them.

In Cibubur, East Jakarta, where Hendropriyono lives, the vicinity never seems to be removed from events in Lampung. Unannounced guests show up, always claiming to know much about Lampung. A friend once joked that Hendro's house was like the local government office for Lampung. He says that they come not only to talk about the Warsidi incident, but about Lampung affairs in general.

A Recluse and a Terrorist

A Report from Major Abdul Azis

On Monday, 6 February 1989, I, Abdullah Makhmud Hendropriyono, at that time a colonel in charge of the *Black Garuda* Military Region Command 043 in Bandar Lampung, had just returned from Palembang to participate in a series of civic action activities. Upon returning, I received a report from Major Abdul Azis that the commander of the military sub-district post, Captain Soetiman, had been detained by a mysterious group at Talangsari III hamlet in Rajabasa Lama village, Way Jepara sub-district. He had been visiting that location along with the head of the Way Jepara sub-district. The visit was being conducted to meet a group which, according to a report prepared by the local community, was led by a person named Warsidi. For the past two years, Warsidi had allegedly been making trouble for the community in the course of his activities conducted in isolation away from the other villagers. Since his arrival, his followers—from Java—had been causing conflicts with the locals.

These new arrivals started to become a physical threat to the hamlet over small issues, such as stealing crops. Because of this, the local community started to ask questions about their presence.

The tension gradually increased until reaching a peak when hamlet chief Sukidi was accosted by five persons bearing knives and machetes. After admitting they were part of Warsidi's gang, they threatened to kill Sukidi. The people of Talangsari III would not put up with such treatment, as they had duly chosen Sukidi as their leader. The community of Rajabasa Lama village joined together with Pakuan Aji, the closest neighboring village, in getting ready to counter any contingencies. At the same time, they reported events to the local authorities and asked them to take measures.

After several summonses by village chief Amir Puspa Mega—who was Sukidi's direct superior—and even after a visit by the sub-district chief, Warsidi was still not properly responding. It was still not clear who comprised his group and what was their purpose. Knowing that Warsidi believed in the motto that the best government leader came from the clerics, the local officials tried to be patient. The head of the Way Jepara sub-district, Zulkifli, headed for Warsidi's house for a second time. This time, he was accompanied by military district commander Major Oloan Sinaga, the police sub-district commander, the village chief of Pakuan Aji, and the hamlet chief of Talangsari III, along with some other local officials and drivers. They used two jeeps and a motorcycle to get to Warsidi's commune in Cihideung. This delegation was attacked by hundreds of people using knives, machetes, and arrows fired from various directions.

The delegation, which had gone there to negotiate and avoid any casualties, was forced to withdraw, leaving Anwar Warsidi's gang to rum amok. These gangs then pursued the delegation, capturing Captain Soetiman and seriously injuring Sergeant Yatin.

Reporting up to the Provincial Military Commander

The report from Major Abdul Azis was passed up the chain of command to the provincial military commander, Major General R. Sunardi. At the time, he was in Bandar Lampung for the opening of a new tennis court for the *Black Garuda* military region command.

Major General Sunardi ordered me to immediately gain the release of Captain Soetiman and pursue efforts to make the vicinity conform with the requests of the locals, who had already submitted their grievances several times to the military district command in Central Lampung.

Village and hamlet chiefs began to contemplate government and military efforts to resolve the growing tension in their area, but they made only slow progress. Therefore, as the situation continued to worsen, the villagers themselves looked to settle matters on their own.

While the community leaders and security officials were conducting a coordination meeting at the residence of the Rajabasa Lama village chief, news was received from the chief of staff of the military region command, Lieutenant Colonel Purbani, that Captain Soetiman had been murdered and his body was being retained by Warsidi's group. He also passed on information that Private Budi Waluyo had been murdered by Warsidi's accomplices in Sidoregjo while he was riding a rented vehicle. The accomplices had fled in the car after its driver, Sabrawi, and his assistant, Matsari, escaped. They had then taken the car to the office of the *Lampung Pos* newspaper in Bandar Lampung and tossed several Molotov cocktails.

Based on this information, it was clear that Warsidi was not in charge of a spiritual group or group studying the Koran. Rather, his people had spread unrest through criminal acts against a wide range of targets.

Such unrest against multiple targets can be defined as terrorism. This becomes even more apparent from their actions on the following day, 7 February 1989, when they conducted a murderous attack against Sidoredjo village chief Santoso Arifin and local police commander Sergeant Sudargo. They also seriously injured police Sergeant Arief Sembering. All three men had been investigating the vehicle theft that took place that night.

Joint Efforts with the Local Populace to Control the Situation

Elements of the provincial and district-level leadership, including myself, took along three platoons of troops and one platoon of the Police Mobile Brigade and moved during the morning of 7 February 1989 to Cihideung and Sidoredjo. We planned to go to Cihideung to confront Warsidid, and to Sideoredjo to put a halt to the terrorism being conducted by the group led by Sugito and Riyanto. At the time, the latter group had possession of two pistols that they had stolen from deceased police Sergeant Sudargo and seriously injured police Sergeant Sembiring.

In the end, physical conflict in Cihideung could not be avoided and Warsidi was killed. On the side of the security forces, some soldiers were seriously injured, including one non-commissioned officer. As had been experienced earlier by the group that included military district commander Oloan Sinaga, Warsidi's followers attacked our contingent; while screaming, they fired poisoned arrows from all directions, including from some guerrillas that had been concealed in chest-deep foxholes. The arrows they used were well made from cyclo tire spokes or bamboo.

This physical clash could not be avoided, as Warsidi's followers screamed and acted like they were possessed. They were all screaming, 'God is great!,' as if they were fighting on behalf of God.

As the situation grew extremely confused and we were using a megaphone to persuade Warsidi's group to halt their opposition, suddenly the huts in the commune began to burn. The troops immediately advanced on the huts, along with locals from Rajabasa Lama, Talangsari III and Pakuan Aji, in an effort to extinguish the flames and save any victims. However, not all of the people could be saved from the fire because those inside threatened their own people and prevented any of them from fleeing. They said, 'Don't go out and surrender to the infidels! We will die together as faithful in here.' So when the fires were burning, many of those who were not brave enough to try to flee died. Among those who were saved was a woman named Widaningsih, who was rescued along with some of her friends by a soldier who braved the flames and went inside.

One of Warsidi's children, Toyibah, jumped out of a window with one of her ears sliced off by a knife by someone inside. She was evacuated and saved after being helped by doctors at the Abdul Malik Hospital.

It was impossible to determine the identities of all of Warsidi's followers, as they had not taken along any identity papers when they arrived. Moreover, many used aliases. For example, Sugito was the alias used by Fadhillah.

It was one of Warsidi's friends who gave testimony that the persons who burned the huts were Warsidi's followers themselves.

The Fury Spreads

On Thursday, 9 February 1989, at about 0900 hours, a group of Warsidi's followers attacked the military district post for Central Lampung. They threw Molotov cocktails from a rented vehicle. The first firebomb hit the motorcycle of Sergeant Kanten, which began to burn. The second one was thrown at the guard post, but it ended up only hitting the signboard and burning the side of the post. At the same time, one of the attackers tried to seize an M-16 automatic rifle from Private Supriadi at the guard post. The guard was seriously injured by able to regain the weapon.

On the same day, the people at the public market in the city of Metro were attacked by a group of Warsidi's followers, who ran amok and stole their goods. The market was subsequently closed for several days after this event.

On the Thursday afternoon, a group of Warsidi's people, armed with machetes and swords, entered the Mardi Waluyo Hospital in Metro. They were searching for members of the armed forces who were hospitalized there. However, they failed because the hospital staff had already taken security precautions. In a clash with a hospital security guard named Kadar, one of the attackers was arrested.

Not all of those who caused turmoil in Lampung since 6 February could be immediately apprehended. Therefore, starting on 8 February, the unrest spread from

Cihideung, Talangsari III and Sidoredjo. As seen from the actions mentioned above, they extended their attacks to Metro in Central Lampung, burning the market and trying to enter the hospital.

To protect and safeguard the people, we conducted coordination meetings with religious and community leaders in order to determine what actions should be taken against Warsidi.

We concluded that Warsidi's movement was a splinter of those who supported the NII concept. This was in line with previous NII actions, but this time they were more cruel and inflicted many casualties, particularly among Muslims.

As a result of the spreading unrest caused by Warsidi, the people throughout Lampung rose up to evict this group. Zaenal Arifin, who was accused of being the Lampung "governor" for the NII movement, was arrested along with his close assistants.

Information obtained from Zaenal Arifin and his accomplices proved that Warsidi had deviated from the larger NII structure. Warsidi had split from the NII at the suggestion of Nurhidayat in Jakarta, who had advocated a separation from Zaenal Arifin.

Nurhidayat is the man most responsible for planning the resultant campaign of heightened cruelty, and did this through Warsidi—an otherwise ordinary man who happened to get 1.5 hectares of land from Jayus in Cihideung.***

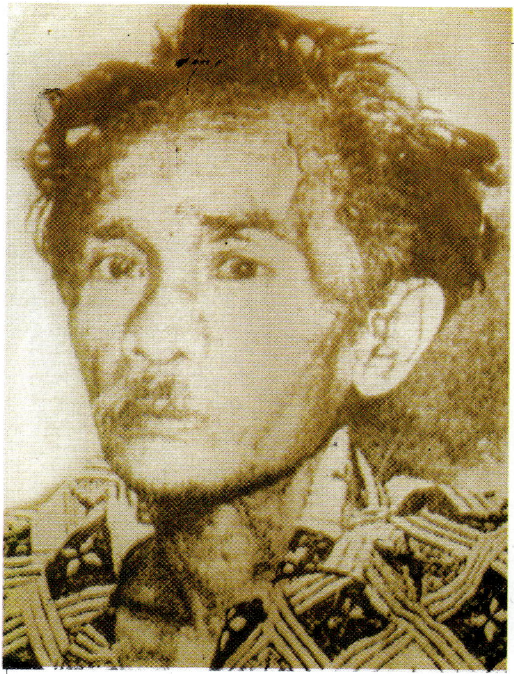

S.M. KARTOSOEWIRJO. A prominent cleric, Kartosoewirjo was the leader of the Darul Islam movement. His broad influence over the Islamic movement in Indonesia continues until the present day.

THE NII PROCLAMATION. In Cisampang hamlet of Cidugaleun village in Leuwisari sub-district of Tasikmalaya, West Java, S.M. Kartosoewirjo proclaimed the NII on 7 August 1949.

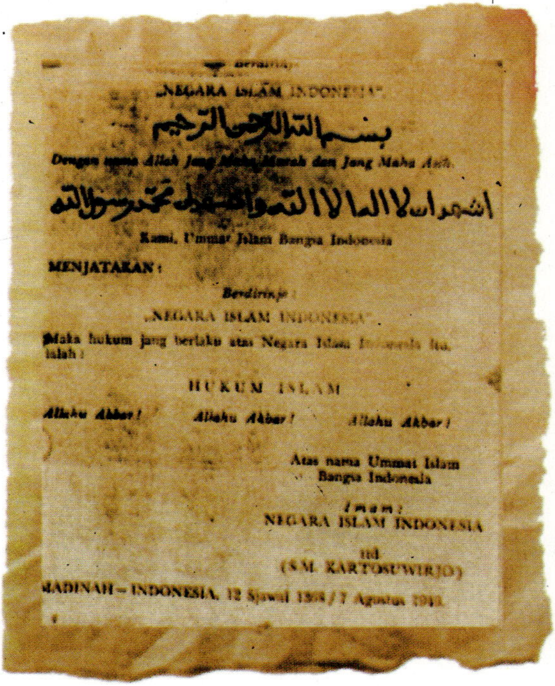

„NEGARA ISLAM INDONESIA"

بسم الله الرحمن الرحيم

Dengan nama Allah Jang Maha Murah dan Jang Maha Asih.

اشهد ان لا اله الا الله واشهد ان محمد رسول الله

Kami, Ummat Islam Bangsa Indonesia

MENJATAKAN :

Berdirinja :

„NEGARA ISLAM INDONESIA".

Maka hukum jang berlaku atas Negara Islam Indonesia itu, ialah :

HUKUM ISLAM

Allahu Akbar! *Allahu Akbar!* *Allahu Akbar!*

Atas nama Ummat Islam
Bangsa Indonesia

Imam :
NEGARA ISLAM INDONESIA

ttd
(S.M. KARTOSUWIRJO)

MADINAH – INDONESIA, 12 Sjawal 1368 / 7 Agustus 1949.

▲ **A.M. HENDROPRIYONO**

The former commander of the Black Garuda Military Region Command 043 in Lampung, Hendropriyono searched across Talangsari hamlet for his subordinate that was murdered by the Warsidi group.

◀

CAPTAIN SOETIMAN

A brave officer, he was a victim of the Warsidi group. He was murdered on Monday, 6 February 1989, by Marsudi (Warsidi's brother).

▲ **ABDUL FATAH WIRANANGGAPATI, 78**. He has carried on S.M. Kartosoewirjo's message from 1949 until the present.

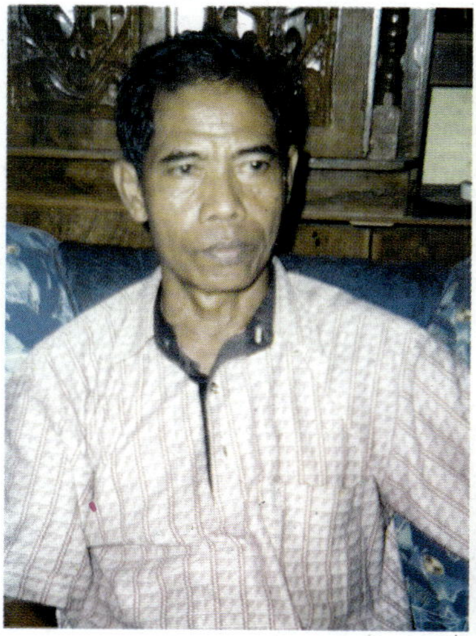

▲ **SUKIDI, 48**. The former chief of Talangsari III hamlet, he was a founder of that hamlet in Rajabasa Lama village in Way Jepara sub-district.

▲ **KH. MUHAMMAD ICHSAN**. He was the leader of the Roudhatul Hidayah boarding school in Mengandung Sari village in Jabung sub-district, East Lampung.

▲ KH. MARZUKI THOHIR, 60.

He was the leader of the Miftakhul Hudda and Miftakhul Fallah boarding schools. He claims that Warsidi built his commune to oppose the goverment.

▲ THE POISONOUS POST

Eleven years ago, this post contained hundreds of poisoned arrows. The author was thankful to find the post still standing before it fell to old age and decay.

▲ **KH. ABU BAKAR BA'SYIR and KH. ABDULLAH SUNGKAR.**
The founder of the Ngruki boarding school in Solo, he escaped to Malaysia after learning that the authorities were moving in for an arrest.

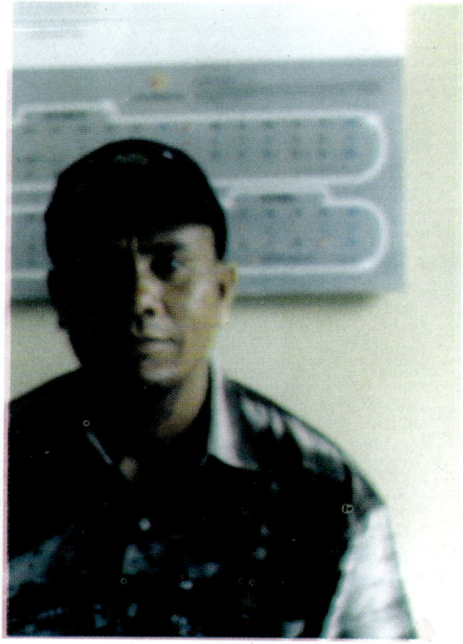

◄

FADHILLAH, 42.
He had an important role in the Central Lampung turmoil. He was the commander of Warsidi's terror group that sowed chaos across Lampung.

▲ **ACHMAD SARIKUN, 60.**
Together with his family in Gedung Wani village, Sarikun was entrusted by Warsidi to lead the base at Gedung Wani.

◀ **SUDARSONO, 38.**
One of the figures behind the Lampung incident, he was the creator of the poisoned arrows.

▶

BENDORIT.
A combination of chopping knife and sickle, this cuts grass and trees equally well. Marsudi used this weapon to cut down Captain Soetiman, which became the trigger for the Talangsari chaos that followed.

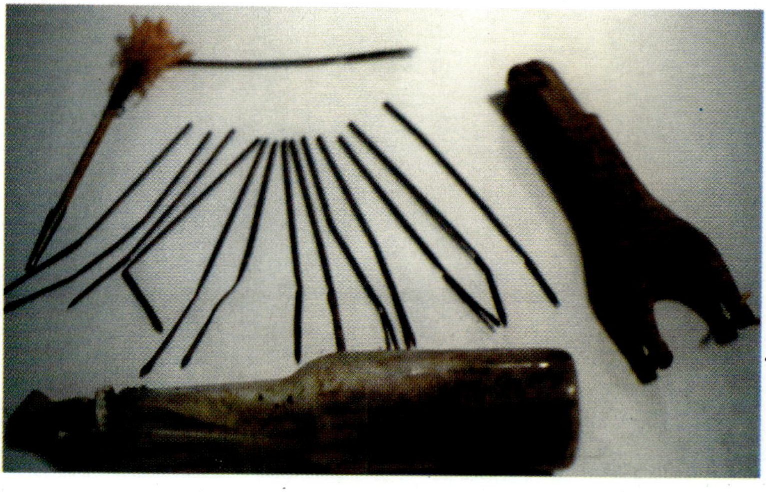

▲ **WEAPONS.**
These poisoned arrows, slingshot, and Molotov cocktail were seized from the Warsidi gang.

▲ **COCONUT TREE BRIDGE.**
This bridge was used to enter the Warsidi commune in Talangsari in 1989. The bridge was made from felled coconut trees. It has now been replaced by a concrete bridge.

▲ **BRIDGE CONSTRUCTED BY MILITARY CIVIC ACTION TEAMS.**
The bridge to Talangsari is now made of concrete. Similar bridges have been built by the army soon after the incident took place.

▲ HISTORIC POST.
This post stands as silent witness to the past. Ten meters beyond this point, Warsidi's gang murdered Soetiman.

▲ THE LOCATION OF THE TURMOIL.
In this place, Warsidi built his commune. Sukidi stands at the exact place where Soetiman was murdered.

▲ **THE MILITARY SUB-DISTRICT POST AT WAY JEPARA, 1999.**
This building stands next to the Way Jepara military sub-district post where Captain Soetiman had his office.

▲ **THE JABUNG POLICE POST, 2000.**
Those at the police post at Jabung Galang Balak were witness to the Gunung Balak incident in 1989.

▲ **CITIZENS' ARREST.**
Locals arrest a member of Warsidi's gang. This is proof that the community had an important role in countering Warsidi's in Talangsari III.

▲ **POISONED ARROWS.**
A batch of seized poisoned arrows. It was these arrows made by Sudarsono that killed Soetiman.

▲ THE WAY JEPARA SUB-DISTRICT OFFICE, 1999.
The distance between the Way Jepara sub-district office and Warsidi's base at Talangsari III was about 12 kilometers.

▲ THE NGRUKI BOARDING SCHOOL, 1989.
The spirit of the NII Islamic State was strongly felt inside the Al-Mukmin boarding school in Ngruki village. This had not been originally intended.

6

CALCULATING FIGURES

What is the meaning of a number?
If words have no meaning, numbers might have any meaning, or they might have no meaning at all. A specific number has certainty assigned to it. He who controls numbers is a most important person.
He who manipulates numbers can get into trouble.

NUMBERS can take on important meaning, especially when several parties begin to dispute a given figure. In the case of the incident at Talangsari in Way Jepara, unrest came about after several people perpetrated a riot. There was a serious upheaval within the Talangsari community when mysterious visitors broke social norms and disturbed the peace. What was initially a small misunderstanding escalated into a major clash. A clash of egos turned into a full-fledged battle. Many people became victims, and many of them died.

Now some people seem to be determined to revisit the Talangsari incident, and they seem to have ulterior motives for certain interest groups. However, the Talangsari community can see through their actions. The community does not trust these interest groups anymore, as they realize they are looking to profit off the events at Talangsari.

Such interest group have frequently tried to peddle their findings to various media outlets more than a decade after the events at Talangsari. Not all of the media trusts their conclusions, however. Among the dozens of domestic media outlets, only a handful have published their news releases. And among those that have published them, they have political motives rather than a real interest in human rights. The smell of the truth and of lies is different, but they try to paper over the lies with alleged humanitarian concerns.

The numbers that have come into question pertain to the victims of the Warsidi gang who caused the turmoil at Talangsari, Way Jepara, Central Lampung, in 1989. When the era of reform came, when the population was no longer afraid of being jailed, some people were euphoric that they could express their opinion without fear. This caused some people to talk about the past, particularly about events at Talangsari that they felt had not been fully settled. It could be that their aim was to present themselves to the community as champions of human rights.

These persons inflated the number of fatalities at the Talangsari incident to 246 persons. This number if far different from the number presented by the local community at the time of the incident.

At that time—just a day after the unrest—the Talangsari community reported to the government that there were 27 fatalities among Warsidi's gang. This number was reported by all of the mass media, both domestically and internationally. Our press did not question the figure. Not until 1998, a decade later, did the issue resurface when a group of people came forward with a new figure.

Some of our media tried to raise the issue again. For example, the 11 October 1998 issue of the *Merdeka Daily* stated that four huts were burned. This paper claimed that each hut was occupied by an average of 100 men, women, and children, and all had died in the fires. This meant that 400 persons had perished. The 22 August 1998 issue of the weekly *Gatra* quoted a figure of 246 civilian fatalities, claiming that four huts, each measuring six by nine meters, had burned down.

Both publications did not saw how the figure could suddenly increase by such a large amount a decade after the incident. How did they arrive at this figure, and what was the reason behind their disclosure of this figure? It is possible that there was never a controversy here. But in reporting such a high figure, suddenly a controversy emerged.

The debate over this figure was actually what motivated this author to write this book. Only this time, the author was determined to get information at the local level, in the Gunung Balak vicinity of Way Jepara (which is now part of East Lampung). The author did not want to estimate the figure or use second-hand reports—he wanted to arrive at a number based on the best possible first-hand information.

Going to the Location

The Cihideung of today is different from the Cihideung of the past, at least in terms of its condition. Now it is overgrown with coarse grass, with leaves blowing in the wind. It is a tranquil place, seemingly without any stress. There are only one or two coconut trees left. They grow high into the sky, as if they want to leave this unmerciful world where the people are cruel. The trees are estimated to be at least twenty years old, perhaps even older. This means that they were silent witnesses to the Talangsari turmoil of over a decade ago. Unfortunately, they cannot speak and give their story.

In coming to the location, the author was overcome by embarrassment. Would he be able to arrive at an accurate casualty figure? Could he come up with a trusted figure that could be defended logically?

As a first step, he worked with the local community to recount the past by using logic. They made a map of the location. Then they added data: what was the area that encompassed Cihideung before it changed to

Talangsari? What were the boundaries of the land Jayus granted to Warsidi? How many houses and huts were on the land granted by Jayus? And how big were those houses and huts that were filled by visitors from various places?

In answering such questions, a number of figures emerged. The total area covered by Cihideung encompasses between 25 and 30 hectares. Within this, Jayus and his family had 5 hectares. From his own land, he granted 1.5 hectares for Warsidi's activities. On this 1.5 hectares of land, Warsidi built a house on stilts measuring six by nine meters for use as his residential house. There were three other huts used as houses for Jayus, Marsudi, and Pardi.

In this area, they intended to establish a commune, with the larger goal of making a Muslim settlement. Their goal changed to developing a base for the NII after a group from Jakarta arrived, including Sudarsono, Nurhidayat, Fauzi, and Wahidin. These four came to Cihideung at the suggestion of Usman, who admits to encouraging them to relocate, and proposed Cihideung in Central Lampung.

This raw data is available to anybody who cares to look. From this data, it is possible to use logic to determine the number of people at the commune. The houses were six by nine meters. It was suggested by some that there might be 100 or more persons in each structure, including husbands, wives, children, in-laws, grandchildren, and even nephews and nieces.

But if that were true, how could they all sleep? Were there facilities to cook for 100 or more persons in each house? Also, how could the commune come up with food for 400 persons each day? It should be noted that this was not a temporary refugee camp. This was Warsidi's commune, a settlement that he planned to occupy for the long-term.

After cross checking with many sources, the actual number of occupants for each house was actually between 25 and 30 persons. Achmad Sarikun, one of Warsidi's former friends, explained that there were 20 to 25 people in Warsidi's house. According to Sarikun's estimate, there were a grand total of about 100 people in the entire commune.

This number sounds logical. When Zulkifli went to Warsidi's house, the sub-district chief said there were between 25 and 30 people present when they threatened to kill him. He recalls that they took up all of the seats that were available. Sukidi, who went to the location several times, confirms Zulkifli's information. When asked if it were possible for each house to have more than 100 people, he said that it would be impossible to live as a normal human being.

Exodus

In trying to calculate the number of people in the commune, one must not forget that there was a large number of people who fled after not wanting to commit themselves to Warsidi. The turmoil took place very fast. There were even some people in the local community who fled because they feared that Warsidi's gangs were going to leave their commune and attack. These people headed into the bush because they saw some of Warsidi's people approaching. In reality, Warsidi's accomplices were just passing through.

At the time, some in the commune heard inner voices telling them not to follow Warsidi anymore because Muslims do not commit murder. They wanted to live. Why did they have to oppose the government, they asked. For many years afterward, the Talangsari community was tainted by the stigma of the fear and crime brought about by Warsidi.

At Pakuan Aji, there was almost the same situation. A day before the incident took place, there was a large exodus of people who left Warsidi's movement. These people were sorry over the murder carried out by the movement. They could not believe that Captain Soetiman was attacked by arrows and machetes until he was killed by Marsudi. Those who disagreed with this action fled their dream commune.

Those in the local community reason that this exodus made the number of people left inside the commune smaller than the original number of occupants. If the original number of occupants was about 100 people, then this number was reduced by the exodus. Sukidi estimates that between 70 to 80 people fled through Talangsari III. Ismed Inonu estimated that about 50 persons passed through Pakuan Aji. These figures do not include those that went to Kelahang.

In the end, it is impossible to exactly calculate the number of victims caused by the Talangsari unrest. When an interest group quotes a figure with certainty, those in the local community know that it must be a lie. The exact number remains a mystery, they know. If one presents a fixed figure that is false, it will surely get that person into trouble.

The version presented by Kontras

The organization Kontras has published a figure that they say is the number of missing persons as a result of the turmoil at Talangsari, Way Jepara, Central Lampung, on 7 February 1989 According to Kontras, based on a report from legal heirs, there were 29 missing persons at Talangsari. These persons were last seen at the Cihideung commune at the Talangsari III hamlet in Rajabasa Lama village, Way Jepara sub-district, in Central Lampung.***

7

Testimony of Loso & Kamarudin

These two witnesses were in the front line of the Talangsari turmoil of 1989. They are from Pakuan Aji, and were selected as guides for the authorities to retake Captain Soetiman's body from Warsidi.

THE deadly Talangsari incident of 1989 cannot be forgotten. Both men still remember how Warsidi was cruel enough to kill his own people when they tried to escape from their burning huts. They cried and screamed from inside the huts, which broke the hearts of Loso and Kamarudin—two witnesses who saw the victims killed by their own leader.

Loso is now 60, while Kamarudin is 30 years old. These two civilians are from Pakuan Aji village, and eleven years ago they were tasked by A. Syarnubi, the village chief from Pakuan Aji, to escort the authorities intent on retaking Captain Soetiman's body from Warsidi's gang at the Cihideung commune in Talangsari II, Way Jepara sub-district of Central Lampung. Loso was to be a guide for Lieutenant Untung, while Kamarudin would accompany Lieutenant Sunarno's team.

Loso, who was a farmer, was entrusted with this role because he was the chief of the Suka Putra III hamlet and really knew the Cihideung area in Talangsari III. The Suka Putra III hamlet of Pakuan Aji directly bordered Cihideung. Therefore, it comes as no surprise that he was chosen to escort the officials who wanted to retake the corpse from the rebel group.

According to Loso, as they approached Warsidi's commune, Untung's team was attacked. Poisoned arrows from Warsidi's hysterical followers began to rain down on them. In the midst of this, Loso heard cries and screams from a house not far from him. The screams were actually from some of Warsidi's members who were butchering their own people who wanted to escape.

Loso, of course, could not do anything in such a situation. From among the victims being butchered, one girl was able to be saved. She was Toyibah, the daughter of Warsidi. She was able to jump from a window, though her ear was cut by a machete while she was still inside. In addition, blood was flowing from her shoulder. Loso quickly gathered her and bundled her back to the authorities, who rushed her to Abdul Muluk Hospital in Bandar Lampung along with several officials who were wounded by poisoned arrows.

Kamarudin, who was entrusted to guide the officials looking to retake Captain Soetiman's corpse from Warsidi, experienced a similar tragic story. Kamarudin was escorting Lieutenant Sunarno's team. At the time, he could directly witness the poisoned arrow attack as the officials got closer to Warsidi's commune.

Their cruelty was not only directed at the authorities. If some of the followers tried to escape, they were pursued and killed as if they were the enemy. Kamarudin could not understand such actions, especially since he was just in his teens. He was also able to see a house containing children who were screaming in fear as flames closed in. The doors were locked and guarded by Warsidi's followers until the fire consumed them all.

This testimony has only recently come to light eleven years after the Talangsari incident. It was not easy to contact these two witnesses. The author twice went to Pakuan Aji in an effort to meet them.

For various reasons, they were unable to meet. Thinking that it was impossible to contact them, the author gave up on both sources.

But when he was actually in the processes of finishing his research, both men—Loso and Kamarudin—submitted two letters of testimony to the chief of Pakuan Aji village attesting to what they witnessed. Their letters follow.***

TESTIMONIAL OF LOSO

Statement of Testimony

The undersigned,

Full name : **Loso,** former chief of Suka Putra III hamlet
Age/Occupation : 60/farmer
Address : Suka Putra III hamlet, Pakuan Aji

I hereby give testimony about which I directly witnessed while joining a team led by Lieutenant Untung to retake the body of Captain Soetiman that was being held by the Warsidi group:

1. I and one friend from Pakuan Aji, Papanto, a man from Suka Putra III hamlet, joined the team.
2. We escorted the team and after getting close to Warsidi's group there was an attack by Warsidi's people. They fired arrows at Lieutenant Untung's group, causing two of Lieutenant Untung's subordinates to be injured by arrows and bullet wounds to their hands.
3. Me and my friend were asked to escort the two victims out of the location to Pakuan Aji.
4. At the time, I heard painful screams. I could see that the screams came from Warsidi's members that were being killed by their own group because they wanted to escape or surrender to the authorities.

This is my statement that is duly recorded to clarify the historical facts during the revolt by Warsidi's group.

At that time, I was still the head of the Suka Putra III hamlet in Pakuan Aji, and I joined with the local community in assisting the team that was countering the Warsidi gang that had made much trouble for us and the surrounding areas.

Pakuan Aji, 15 May 2000

[signed]

Loso

TESTIMONIAL OF KAMARUDIN

Statement of Testimony

The undersigned:

Full name : Kamarudin
Age/Occupation : 30/Farmer
Address : Pakuan Aji

I hereby give testimony that I directly witnessed when I joined a team led by Lieutenant Sunarno that was looking to retake Captain Soetiman's corpse that was being held by Warsidi.

1. I escorted the team upon the instruction of the late village chief A. Sarnubi Aji.
2. When the team approached Warsidi's commune, Warsidi's people fired arrows at us.
3. I personally saw people from Warsidi's group that wanted to escape or surrender killed by their own group.
4. I also personally saw a house full of children hysterically screaming. Warsidi's group burned the house. Warsidi's people guarded the front and back doors as the house burned down.

My statement is duly recorded to clarify the historical facts about the Warsidi revolt.

Pakuan Aji, 15 May 2000
[signed]

Kamarudin

8

The Story of the Poisoned Arrows

In a dream word, anything can happen.
Some things are impossible in the real world,
but are very possible in dreams.
Nothing is impossible in dreams.
Anything can happen.
Everything is easy.

WHEN there is a war in the Javanese shadow puppet theater, those who are involved can use all kinds of weapons. Warriors can employ arrows and keris, while their opponents can use all sorts of daggers, lances, and machetes to kill.

An arrow is used to kill an enemy from a far distance, while the keris is employed for close-in fighting. Both are considered good weapons. Some allegedly had miraculous origins, like coming from the teeth of a demigod. The best mythical weapons came directly from the gods.

In general, the gods in the puppet theater gave arrows to descendents of Pandawa because Pandawa was known to be an expert in worship and meditation. These arrows came with various powers. Some of the arrows supposedly came with miraculous powers. For example, one was supposed to be able to change its appearance. Another was able to emit light in the darkness.

The best of all weapons was the *carka*, an arrow used by the royal warrior Kresna (also known as Arjuna). It was the most honored and feared of all weapons. The cakra came with all sorts of powers. According to myth, Arjuna wanted to gain possession of a cakra, which was used by the god Wisnu and was not supposed to be given to mere mortals. Disguising himself as a giant who was the descendent of Wisnu, Arjuna was able to get this special weapon.

During the mythical Baratayuda War, Arjuna used his cakra. It had many special powers. When the arrow was fired into the sky, for example, it could nearly reach the Sun. The Earth would begin to shake and the afternoon turned dark as night.

This tactic was used when Arjuna swore he would burn himself alive if he could not defeat the evil Jayadrata. Upon hearing that vow, Jayadrata hid so that Arjuna could not find him. This ploy failed, however, because the clever Arjuna fired a cakra into the air and turned day into night. When Jayadrata came out to investigate, he was hit by an arrow and killed. After that, Arjuna never again eclipsed the Sun with his cakra. The Earth regained its earlier brightness, and evil left the world along with Jayadrata. This is, of course, just the world of the imagination.

Poisoned Arrows

Sudarsono of course had no connection with Dursasono, the perpetually happy warrior that lived in the mythical Kurawa land of Astinapura. Darsono was not dreaming of such myths when he decided to fashion some arrows—arrows that were destined to cause much trouble. An ethnic Javanese born in Belawan, Medan, he was just 26 years old when his arrows caused deaths. Until now, he has never shown any sorrow for what he created. He has even hinted that he is proud for upholding his religious convictions.

According to Sudarsono, the Prophet Muhammad called for Muslims to learn martial arts, swimming, firing arrows, and riding horses. Although such an interpretation of the Prophet's words are questioned by many people, Darsono taught his followers how to make bows and arrows. It does not matter if the interpretation was right or wrong: what is important is that Darsono understood this as God's instructions.

The arrows he made were indeed uncommon. Not only were they fashioned from unique materials—the spokes from a cyclo—but their form was also unusual. They were not more than 30 centimeters in length. The sharp end was formed into a point from a material like tin. The tail was made from seven pieces of rope, which were combed out to be fibrous. To fire these arrows, Darsono made bows with lengths of rubber that could be stretched back for an entire arm's length. Using this arrow, the arrow could be fired to a distance of about 200 meters.

The public would have never known of these arrows if they had not caused such trouble. The term 'poisoned arrows' suddenly became well known after word of Warsidi's revolt spread. Some initially doubted news of these arrows. This was because when Sergeant Yatin was hospitalized, no evidence of poison was found by the doctors who treated him.

However, Sudarsono has confirmed the fact that poison was used. He has revealed how the cyclo spokes became a deadly weapon. Initially, this was not his intention. But his accomplices, and also his superior (Nurhidayat, alias Amir Musafir), urged him to make the arrows.

Meantime, Alex, Sudarsono's friend from Tanjung Priok, claimed to know how to make poison from a tree resin. Alex claimed that the resin could only be obtained through a special ritual and only by certain people.

First, the resin has to be taped from the tree. After the resin has dried, it is made into a powder. Then the tips of the arrows are dipped into the powder to become poisoned arrows. When the tips have been poisoned, they are covered by small plastic shields to prevent the user from himself being poisoned. In the past, this poison was used to kill such animals as pigs, rhinos, and elephants.

According to Darsono, most of the poisoned arrows were made in Jakarta. Alex and some of his friends continued producing them in Lampung. Before a very large number had been produced, the turmoil broke out. Sudarsono believes that not more than one thousand arrows had been made until that time. The arrows exported to Lampung were used against Captain Soetiman, the military sub-district chief, who was later killed by Warsidi's brother, Marsudi.

That is the story of the poisoned arrows. They were the creation of Sudarsono, who claimed to be following the Prophet's instructions to learn to fire arrows, ride a horse, practice martial arts, and swim. This should be a lesson for all of us when it comes to being wise in understanding the good instructions contained within Islam.***

9

THE SPIRITUAL MOVEMENT IN LAMPUNG

The will to find God
is not a monopoly of one group or individual.
It is not confined to a specific time or place.
This will may rise up at any time or any place.
Problems come when this will differs between
different places and different persons.
This is why people have devoted themselves
to spiritual life for ages.
Not just now—but during all eras.

IF one looks for God, finding Him is a certainty. This is because there is no creature that does not spring from Him. Whether this is accepted or rejected, realized or avoided, the fact is that at the end of life, all creatures pass on. They have originated from God, and they will return to God.

All creatures are actually existing in the same space, just different places. We are not going to leave Him. We merely return to Him. He is the God of the entire Universe. And we are the spiritual actors who run toward our origin. The only difference is the way we perform our spiritual observances. Such observances determine the quality of the actor, whether he is of high quality or low, an angel or a devil. Those of good quality are qualified to meet God. Those who are not of good quality and just follow others will be confused and deviate from the desired path.

Often times, a highly spiritual person talks in a louder voice, and sometimes claims that there is no other truth than what he or his group represents. He has the 'best' truth. Such groups will often have problems with other persons, and with themselves.

Lampung is not only a city known for its peppers, but also for its spirituality. History shows that many religions have gone there and stayed a long time. Banten came with its Islamic influence, Sriwijaya brought Hinduism, and Christianity came with the Europeans. All of these beliefs colored the spiritual life of the locals down to the village level. The following data lists the spiritual groups that have prospered in South Sumatra.***

A List of Spiritual Groups in Lampung

Spiritual Name	Location	Remarks
Ilmu Sejati	Pringsewu, Metro, and Gedongtaan	Defunct since June 1996
Peguyuban Penglawan Ilmu Kebatinan	Metro	Defunct since the G30S coup of September 1965
Sapto Darmo	Metro and Gedongtaan	Being monitored
Kaweruh Naluri	Metro and Pringsewu	Being monitored
Ngesti Rahayu	Metro	No longer active
Darulhadist	Metro	Changes name, constantly monitored
Imam Mahdi	Terbanggi Besar	No further information
Ilmu Hizib Adam dan Tarekat	Metro	Under investigation
Semedi	Metro (shaman)	Not active

Agama Islam Hakekat	Metro	Dissolved after G30S
Pran Soeh	Metro	Dissolved by the Central Lampung district government in May 1969
Lelampahan	Metro	Known since September 1970
Parisada Hindu Dharma	Seputih Raman	Established on 31 July 1965 for Hindus from Bali
Lembaga Bayangkara	Tanjung Karang	No more followers
Agama Buddha Jawi Wisnu Indonesia	Metro	Under investigation
Yayasan Amaliah Pondok Islam	Tanjung Karang	Active and being monitored
Ahmadiah	Telukbetung	Active
Khawatiyah-Samadiyah	Telukbetung	Active
Gerakan Ratu, aka Paksi Pak Batok	Gedongtaan	Prohibitied by South Lampung authorities since 24 September 1968

Jemaah Muslimin	Pringsewu	Being monitored
Tarikat Naksabandiyah	Central Lampung	Active
Islam Putih	Central Lampung	Not-active
Islam Sejati	Central Lampung	Prohibited by Pringsewu state prosecutor, March 1973
Jemaah Mujahidin Fisabilillah, Sempalan Darul Islam	Central Lampung	Banished by the government since February 1989

10

About the Islamic State

There is no use of force in Islam.
In actuality, it is clear
which is the right way
and which is the wrong way.

ISLAM has never forced people to live according to Islamic precepts or any other ways. It allows Islam and other religions. Islam has also never required people to live under an Islamic government. This is because it makes clear which is the right way and the wrong way for its believers. This shows that Islam is not spread by force, or in a cruel way. Islam is not spread by the blade of a sword or in bloody fashion.

Reality, however, is sometimes contrary to this. Many in the world believe that Islam is spread through negative means. Invasions, attacks, and weapons are used against those that do not accept Islam. Actually,

Islam teaches that one enemy is too many, and a thousand friends too little. The Prophet Muhammad always told his followers to introduce Islam by showing compassion, that each must show their inner beauty through good behavior. These are the true weapons for each Muslim, he said.

As the Koran confirms, the existence of Islam is to take human beings from a state of stupidity to freedom, from darkness to light. Islam is to change thinking and behavior from stupidity to glory, from cruelty to being civilized.

History shows that Islam has contributed much to improving the quality of life. Its existence has made clear the journey of human beings from era to era. It has saved the Earth from the threat of darkness, and made it civilized. It has shown a good way of life for all people.

Arnold Toynbe, in his book *Dakwah to Islam*, said that the behavior of Muslims is beloved by followers of other religions. He said that when the Moslem troops led by Abu Ubaidah came to the Urdu, a Christian staying there wrote a letter to Arabian Moslems:

"Greetings to All Moslems, you are more beloved that the Romans, even though they have the same religion as us. You are more dedicated, and worthy of respect. But the Romans have conquered us and our Earth."

This shows their feeling that they are happier in welcoming Moslems than the Romans. The people in cities lived in fear and closed their doors in order to avoid the Roman soldiers that looked to plunder their properties and hurt them.

The Indonesian Islamic State

The above story is an example that shows Islam does not inspire fear, nor is it a threat. Islam is appropriate to be a leading belief because it is capable of accommodating all people and protecting all religions. This is the basis why an Islamic State has become a divine goal for some people. They believe that Islam will protect all people from suffering, whatever their color, creed, or language. Islam will make clear their lives in this world and the hereafter.

History has recorded that the Prophet fourteen centuries ago established Darul Islam, or the Madinah State. The Prophet Muhammad visited there, and the people supported his precepts. They supported his struggle without physically following him as he continued his mission.

Madinah became Darul Islam, led directly by the Prophet. He was a Moslem leader at that time. Under his leadership, the physical and spiritual glory of human beings began to shine. Many people believe that this was the golden age of human beings. This was the only time when the Prophet led his people. Now a similar golden age is expected by all human beings. Many await this period to come again in the future. They are waiting for the second coming of the Prophet.

Indonesia has also known Darul Islam, the name given to a movement to establish an Indonesian Islamic State (abbreviated as NII) under S.M. Kartosoewirjo. This founder of Darul Islam wanted to realize the Prophet's aim of establishing Madinah State. Kartosoewirjo wanted to apply the same tactics used by the Prophet in establishing an Islamic government to protect the interests of Islam. In Cisampang hamlet, Cidugaleun village, Keuwisari sub-district, Tasikmalaya, West Java, on 7 August 1949, S.M. Kartosoewirjo proclaimed NII. He did this even though it was to cause challenges and problems from that time through the present—and no doubt into the future.***

PROCLAMATION ESTABLISHING THE INDONESIAN ISLAMIC STATE

Bismillahirrahmanirrahim

Asjhadoe anla ilahailallah wa asjhadoe anna Moehammadar Rasoeloellah

We, Indonesian Moslems declare:

The Establishment of an **INDONESIAN ISLAMIC STATE**

That the prevailing law in the Indonesian Islamic State shall be **ISLAMIC LAW**

God the Greatest! God the Greatest! God the Greatest!

On behalf of Indonesian Moslems

THE LEADER OF THE INDONESIAN ISLAMIC STATE

[*signed*]

S.M. KARTOSOEWIRJO

MADINAH INDONESIA

12 Sjawal 1368 H. / 7 August 1949

11

THE DARUL ISLAM MOVEMENT

Darul Islam has been banished. Its followers have been eliminated. Those imprisoned were later given amnesty by the Indonesian government in 1962.

BUT Darul Islam still exists. They call themselves the followers of DI, an organization of former DI-TII members that were previously killed off or given amnesty. They move like the wind, invisible to the eye but always there. They use missionary methods as their tactic. Through missionary activities, their goal of establishing an Indonesian Islamic State can be kept alive.

Their missionary movement has been silent but effective. They are constantly bringing in new members. The senior members of the movement decide who is loyal and qualified to be a new NII member. Sometimes, the appointing seniors have no direct links to the DI leaders of the past.

Darul Islam originated from the words Dar Al Islam. Literally translated, this means 'House of Islam,' 'Family of Islam,' or the 'Peace Family.' In a more broad interpretation, it means an 'Islamic Zone' or 'Islamic State.'

At its core, however, the meaning of Darul Islam has the word 'Islam,' and it implies that the Islamic way must be carried out. The opposite of Darul Islam is Darul Harb, which means 'War Territory' or 'World of the Infidels' who must be brought into Darul Islam.

The reality of the Islamic movement throughout the world has been that whenever Muslims encounter difficulties and try to assert themselves, the interpretation of Darul Islam become extreme. In Indonesia, Darul Islam became a desire to create an Indonesian Islamic State through force and cruelty.

Ironically, Moslems supporting Darul Islam began to revolt only in areas where they constituted the majority of the population. They then began to conduct changes through harsh methods. It should be noted that the reasons behind the birth of Darul Islam in Indonesia differed from area to area.

In Aceh, for example, Darul Islam arose because of religious demands. In South Sulawesi, it came about as a result of the demobilization of former guerrillas after 1950. In South Kalimantan, the movement was a result of low self-esteem after being neglected for a long period. In West Java and Central Java, it came about due to social inequalities.

The Muslims in Indonesia were wronged by both the government as well as a number of political parties. Problems arose from the state ideology, from the role and structure of the armed forces, as well as the authority of the central government and the lagging socio-economic development in rural areas All of these factors contributed to the birth of the Darul Islam movement.

Early in the independence struggle, Islamic leaders participated in the debate over the constitution in 1945 and the state ideology of Pancasila. They also acknowledged that the republic was the sole legal state. In reality, they expected that Indonesia would become an Islamic state after the defeat of the Dutch. They believed that Darul Islam would come about. But the concept of establishing an Islamic state was sidetracked—and then boomeranged back to disturb the formation of the Republic of Indonesia.

The result was that Darul Islam tried to establish an Indonesian Islamic State. The only movement in the beginning was the Darul Islam movement in West Java, where S.M. Kartosoewirjo on 7 August 1949 proclaimed the NII. This movement later spread to Central Java, South Kalimantan, South Sulawesi, and Aceh. The spread of DI then went as far as the Nusa Tenggara island, Maluku, and Halmahera.

In several of these areas, the Darul Islam movement made many advances over a long period. Not until the 1960s was the Indonesian armed forces able to eliminate these various revolts.

In West Java, the end of the movement came in 1962. In South Kalimantan, it came in 1963, and in South Sulawesi in 1965. By contrast, the rebellion in Central Java ended in 1955; in Aceh, where disturbances did not break out until 1953, the trouble was harder to quell. A compromise was reached in Aceh in 1957, and the final rebels surrendered in 1962.

The Fall of Darul Islam

Internationally, Darul Islam got no support. Even the Islamic state in the Middle East did not offer help. In the rare cases where interest was show, it was limited to a few individuals and remained small. For example, Van Kleev, an ex-Dutch soldier who converted to Islam, said he sympathized with Darul Islam and tried to help them through diplomatic means. Through letters sent to the U.S. and other nations, he was fairly successful in alerting foreign audiences to the DI cause. However, until the end of the DI movement, no foreign nation ever offered support.

The fall of Darul Islam was accelerated by several factors. First, there was the government policy that called on the military to immediately eradicate the various revolts. Second, second senior DI leaders decided to rally, such as Hasan Saleh in Aceh and Bahar Mattaliu in South Sulawesi. Third, the movement lacked weapons and had low morale.

Another important factor was the fact that the various rebel factions were scattered. Even among Muslims, DI was considered a threat to national disintegration. Darul Islam, moreover, conducted many atrocities, including some by Kartosoewirjo.

In the end, only small groups like Hisbullah and Sabilillah remained at large.

Masyumi leaders, such as M. Natsir, who earlier were sympathetic to the Islamic state, turned away from the DI movement. The 'wall of feet' strategy used by the armed forces was finally successful in rounding up the last DI holdouts.

Even though DI had been physically eliminated, it would later rise again during the New Order government. The last chapter in the history of the DI movement had yet to be written.***

12

A SPLINTER OF DARUL ISLAM

AFTER Sekarmadji Maridjan Kartosoewirjo, the person who proclaimed the Indonesian Islamic State, passed away, the leadership of the NII movement was held by Kahar Muzakkar until 1965. It was then passed to Daud Beureueh through 1980. However, after leadership passed from these original leaders and was set to go to the next generation, conflicts of opinion and misunderstandings arose as to who should be the proper leader of the movement.

During 1978–79, Darul Islam broke into two wings. The first, Jamaah Fillah, was chaired by Djadja Sujadi. The second, Jamaah Sabilillah, was chaired by Adah Djaelani Tirtapradja. Both were the most senior military leaders in the DI, having been directly appointed by Kartosoewirjo as members of his high command. The two leaders then clashed with each other, and Djadja Sujadi was killed by Adah Djaelani.

Adah Djaelani was jailed in 1980 and disputes within his Jamaah Sibilillah broke out. As a result, Darul Islam dissolved into several smaller groups, each with their own chairman. Unfortunately, these groups did not recognize or cooperate with each other.

In this chaos, there was one group under Abdullah Sungkar that had a fair amount of influence. His power base was in Central Java, especially around Solo and Yogyakarta. This group established the Ngruki boarding school in Solo as a center for training leaders, who could then be sent out to win more followers. Many of these cadre members spread across Indonesia in an attempt to revive DI. Some of them are the ones that went to Talangsari, Cihideung, Lampung, and later joined with Warsidi.

Among the groups under Abdullah Sungkar was the Atjent Kurnia group, which covered Bogor, Serang, Purwakarta, and Subang, and the Ajengan Masduki group that was active in Jakarta and Lampung. The members of these groups were not only trained in religious matters, but also in military topics. Their instructors included those who had fought with the Mujahidin in Afghanistan.

Among the leaders during this period was an old man named Abdul Fatah Wirananggapati. He still had a relatively large number of followers spread across many areas. As an older leader, he had been the person responsible for spreading the idea of DI to Aceh when Kartosoewirjo was still alive.

Within DI, there was another leader named Gaos Taufik, who had much influence in Sumatra. The followers of Gaos were prepared to become 'soldiers of God' in Sumatra in order to spark a rebellion in Indonesia. This group was said to have close ties with the Moro liberation front in the Philippines and the Pattani mujahidin in Thailand.

In the 1990s, there was an ideological dispute within Darul Islam. At the time, Adah Djaelani delegated his authority to Abu Toto (alias Toto Salam). According to some informed sources, Toto Salam had never been a recognized DI member, yet he always used the concept of NII. He continued the traditions of Darul Islam, and allegedly controlled about 50,000 followers. Under his leadership, the huge Al-Zaytun boarding school was constructed in Mekar Jaya village, Haurgeulis, Indramayu, West Java. This project covered thousands of hectares and sparked the jealously of other Darul Islam leaders.

Since that time, morale within the Darul Islam movement collapsed. Its unity has broken down due to competing egos. The Indonesian public has come to know that Darul Islam is led by unqualified people.

Wirananggapati and Abdullah Sungkar

These two Darul Islam leaders were indirectly involved in the Talangsari incident. In researching this topic, the author was able to meet with them. The following is a profile of both leaders.

Abdul Fatah Wirananggapati

A student who wanted to become a soldier, he still possesses Kartosoewirjo's letter of proclamation. Abdul Fatah Wirananggapati professes to be a pure Darul Islam leader. He notes that, until this time, he has never surrendered. Born in Kuningan in 1923 and of advanced age, he still speaks of Darul Islam as though it has never gone. Such beliefs are contained within a tall and slender man, a man who is more concerned with the contents in his head than his stomach. He is still fit, with his feet moving as fast as his speech.

His goal to be a soldier was achieved when he met S.M. Kartosoewirjo in the jungle of Loyang, Jatibarang, West Java, in 1951. At that time, Kartosoewirjo was mobilizing forces to defend the establishment of the NII that he had proclaimed. Kartosoewijro then appointed Wirananggapati as a member of the NII military with the rank of colonel. Such a high rank was hard to obtain, even for persons who had been close to Kartosoewirjo. This made other cadre members jealous, such as Adah Djaelani, Haji Abidin, and Ajengan Masduki. Adah Djaelani was a member of the NII high command, and had been a witness when Kartosoewirjo proclaimed the establishment of NII.

Not only did Kartosoewirjo make Abdul Fatah Wirananggapati a colonel, but he also made him a representative of the High Command, which was equivalent to a High Command member or the head of the general staff. In certain situations, this meant that Wirananggapati might represent or even replace Kartosoewirjo.

The following are quotes from an interview with Wirananggapati.

As a representative of the High Command, what were your tasks?

I was a mediator at home and abroad. Although I had a mandate for diplomatic tasks abroad, I had to first manage domestic affairs. It is nonsense if the affairs in the home country had not yet been managed. Therefore, I immediately consulted with Islamic leaders in the local area who professed similar beliefs. In Aceh, there was Daud Beureueh, a local leader who was respected by both the government and his own followers. I met him and explained about the NII that Kartosoewirjo had proclaimed on 7 August 1949.

What are your comments about Daud Beureueh?

Before I met him, he said that he wanted to conduct a revolt against the Republic of Indonesia. I told him that an NII had already been established, so why doesn't he join the NII proclaimed by Kartosoewirjo. If he conducted a revolt by joining the NII, he would not have to be subject to secular law. Hearing this, he was happy and agreed to support the NII. He immediately was appointed as commander of the NII's 5 Division. At the same time, the government sent delegations to Aceh to pursue Daud Beureueh, but they were not successful. This was because he had joined the NII.

Why did you go to Aceh first and not other region?

Because Aceh was an Islamic region. For diplomatic purposes, Aceh was closer and easier to reach by diplomatic interests abroad. For example, if we wanted to go to Malaka, Penang, Trenggano, Johor, or Negeri Sembilan in Malaysia, Aceh would be an effective staging ground. Aceh became a priority because Daud was prepared to conduct a secular attack against the government. Fortunately, it did not occur and he joined with the NII.

After that, where did you go?

Back to Jakarta. I wanted to come back by myself, but that was not allowed. A commander must be guarded, Daud said. In returning to Jakarta, I was accompanied by Major Ilyas Lebai on the instruction of Daud. I was brought to Hasan Gayo's house in Mangga Besar II, Jakarta. In fact, Hasan Gayo was a spy for the government and quietly reported me. I was arrested.

After several days of investigation, I was accused of conducting political crimes. All documents were seized as evidence. I was jailed at Nusakambangan until 1962.

Who else from DI was captured?

All DI troops supporting Kartosoewirjo were arrested, including Adah Djaelani. After Kartosoewirjo was arrested, the situation became unstable. I was ordered to surrender, but I did not do it. Eventually, they forgot about me. When Ali Murtopo gave out the spoils of the New Order to close the mouths of DI members, I was not asked to join. Those DI members who surrendered were generally rich. This includes Adah Djaelani, who has his own company and a big apartment in Jakarta.

After being released from Nusakambangan, what did you do?

I went back to the community to be a teacher of the Koran. This is different from the others, like Danu, Ateng, H. Abidin, and others, who became businessmen. According to me, DI must struggle through better behavior and more knowledge. Therefore, I prefer to be a teacher of the Koran. This will allow future DI leaders to be better qualified.

How about the current young leaders of DI?

They have good spirit, but they must watch their behavior. For example, Nurhidayat. If he had been able to maintain good behavior, he would have been a good cadre member. He must apologize. He has made many difficulties for others due to his actions in Lampung in 1989. I had prohibited him from taking action in Lampung, but he went ahead anyway. In the end, many people got into trouble, especially those who visited him in Bandung. They were my students, and all of them were arrested.

Why did you prohibit Nurhidayat's group from going to Lampung?

If they were to go to Lampung, they had to have a good reason and clear rules of behavior. What will they do in Lampung? Why conduct actions there? Who is their leader? I do not know him. We must increase our knowledge, not prepare for war. The person behind the Lampung commotion was Nurhidayat, who influenced Warsidi. Nurhidayat is an ambitious man. Because of the Talangsari turmoil, I, too, was arrested as a DI leader behind Nurhidayat.

Are you proud to be an NII leader?

Of course, because NII not only belongs to Darul Islam, but all Muslims. Look at the text of its proclamation. It is written that NII is on behalf of all Muslims. The problem for me is not about its name, but about the applicability of Islamic law.

Who is actually entitled to replace Kartosoewirjo?

Actually, there are laws and articles of association for NII. If a cleric becomes incapacitated, the candidates to replace him must be qualified. They are taken from the High Command, or the representative of the High Command. Among them, one must chose the most senior. According to me, Adah Djaelani is the most appropriate. But he has surrendered to the government. Therefore, the selection must be limited to those that did not surrender. Kiai Masduki is also appropriate because he is also an old leader. Moreover, he has memorized the Koran, but his behavior is not that good for a cleric. For example, in front of others he has said that I am appropriate to be a cleric, but behind my back he tries to arrange power for himself. This is not good or correct. Finally, there is a conflict and DI split into three groups. Adah Djaelani went with the Toto Abu Salam group, Tachmid went with Mia Ibrahim, and Ajengan Masduki went with Gaos Taufik. Daud Beureueh had appointed Gaos.

How many NII supporters are there now?

I don't know. As far as ideological supporters, I think this covers almost all Muslims. They are waiting for the enforcement of Darul Islam. Actually, there are still many others, like Suryanegara Mansyur. He is an NII leader.

Abdullah Sungkar

Kiai Abdullah Sungkar has special characteristics that have influenced his students and followers. He never says something is right if he knows it is wrong. The Soeharto government grew confused over his statements, which some saw as too strict and too extreme.

One early morning in a small mosque east of the Kusumoyudan complex in Tjokroaminoto University in Surakarta, an Islamic teacher with great energy spoke to a gathering of not more than eight people. Starting from a small leased space, there is something that can grow big, he said. He was referring to the mosque, where the mosque leaders had many times in the past apologized for the light attendance during the morning lecture.

On another occasion, this teacher, along with his wife and child, had been in a dormitory for the blind. In the dormitory, he had brought breakfast for the blind people while he preached in his energetic style. He always spoke in fiery terms, no matter on what occasion or how many people he was addressing. This man was K.H. Abdullah Sungkar, an NII figure who was well built with white skin. His words always got a rise, and he always spoke his mind.

Some people felt that Abdullah Sungkar's speeches were dangerous. He never hesitated to criticize the government at a time that no one dared to voice such sentiment. For Sungkar, one must always say the truth, even if one is to be imprisoned on many occasions. That is why whenever he made a speech, it was attended not only by his followers but also by intelligence officers.

And that is why Abdullah Sungkar was censored whenever he wrote anything. Small wonder that he was monitored by the authorities.

Together with Abu Bakar Ba'syir, he established the Al-Mukmin boarding school in South Solo, in early 1973. An elementary school and a radio station were also established. His boarding school grew fast, as did the radio station. Although the Ngruki boarding school was successful, Abdullah Sungkar's luck was running out.

In planning for the arrest of Abdullah Sungkar at the Ngruki boarding school, several officers kept watch. Others entered the school to make the arrest. It was later learned that he wore a sarung and escaped through the gate on a motorcycle, right past the watchful eyes of the security officials. Once out of the boarding school, he took a bus to Jakarta.

That was his last day in Solo, and his last day at the Al-Mukmin boarding school that he built in Ngruki. It was a fantastic escape. From a location within Malaysia, he told the author that he only had

Rupiah 10,000 in his shirt pocket. With this small amount, he went to Jakarta, then to Pekanbaru in Riau, and finally crossed the border to Malaysia.

There is another version to this story. Prior to leaving for Malaysia, the Condet group—which he built and was under his influence—hid Abdullah Sungkar. This group consisted of the new NII generation, including Aus Hidayat, Ibnu Thoyyib, Haryono, Dodi Achmad Busubul, Mukhliansyah, and Nurhidayat. This last person had been chosen in 1988 by Musafir to go from Jakarta to build a base at Cihideung and Talangsari. Their friends included Sudarsono, Fauzi Isnan, Sukardi, Maulana Latif, Alex, and Joko, all of who kept in touch with those at Warsidi's commune at Cihideung in Lampung.

In Malaysia, Abdullah Sungkar lived in exile away from big cities. He stayed in rural areas with only a small number of followers. He was then joined by Abu Bakar Ba-asyir, his co-founder of the Al-Mukmin boarding school. They both then blended among the farmers in rural Malaysia.

It was not easy to track these fugitives. In Malaysia, they were protected by the local authorities. Only through the help of A. Halim Abbas and Helmi Al-Mascaty from the Al-Arqam Malaysia community was the author able to meet them.

The author drove in a car from Kuala Lumpur to Negeri Sembilan. Passing through forests and a number of villages, they stopped at a hut beside a small alley. It was approaching sunset, and the writer was able to see two men with gray beards and moustaches pulling a small cart filled with agricultural tools. These were the two leaders from Ngruki that he sought.

Abdullah Sungkar opened the conversation by quoting the Koran. He said that he only asked the government for a small thing. He wanted a place, only a small island, to build a commune that might become a model Islamic village. He said he did not believe it when he heard the government had changed. When told that the Habibie government had freed all leftist and rightist prisoners, he said that he did not believe it.

Several days after this meeting, both men went to the airport with their briefcases. They took a moment to have their photographs taken before heading to Saudi Arabia.

Since then, the name of Abdullah Sungkar has not been repeated by many people. In early 2000, he secretly went back to Indonesia. He spent only a few months in Bogor before he grew ill and died.***

13

NGRUKI AND TALANGSARI

FOR many people outside of Solo, Central Java, it is not easy to spell the word Ngruki, and the name does not hold any meaning. But in that village, there is an Islamic study group and a boarding school named Al-Mukmin. In that place, many Muslim cadre members have been trained. They have spread to many places, including Warsidi's commune in Cihideung, Talangsari III, Way Jepara, Central Lampung.

Abdullah Sungkar and Abu Bakar Ba'asyir established the Al-Mukman boarding school around 1973. Both were clerics in Central Java. Initially, the school was in a mosque on Sukohardjo Street in the southern part of Solo. Besides the boarding school, the complex also had a radio station named Radis (for *Radio Dakwah Islam*). At that time, it was the only non-profit radio station competing with dozens of commercial stations like ABC, Rama, PTPN, Panca, and others.

Though it was non-profit, Radis was able to support itself by donations, including some from fanatic listeners. The station broadcast nothing but Islamic themes, including speeches by Abdullah Sungkar, religious quotations, and Malay songs. The radio station survived without any commercials.

Except for female broadcasters, all Radis employees had to attend nightly lectures held by the boarding school leaders. The substance of their Islamic study was to discuss Islamic teachings, its rules, history, and how to implement those rules based on the Prophet's teachings. These lessons were assisted by several clerics, including Kiai Hasan Basri, Amir S.H., Abdullah Thofel, and others from Solo.

This was the Ngruki Islamic study group, later known as the Usroh study group, that later came to be questioned by both the government and followers of Sungkar. The group grew very fast and was soon known everywhere.

Because of its fast growth, it outgrew its initial location. Therefore, they began looking for a new site. Every day, the Al-Mukmin boarding school became overcrowded with followers. In early 1974, the location moved to Ngruki, the name of a hamlet in Tipes village, nor far from the Solo bus terminal in the eastern part of the city.

Upon moving to the new location, Radis radio and Sungkar's Islamic group started to grow hostile toward the local authorities. The government regarded Sungkar as too vocal in his criticisms. It seemed like the government found the situation growing too risky, and wanted to make an example of the cleric and his followers.

Accordingly, Sungkar was slowly squeezed. It even began to look like he was going to be arrested. Sungkar did not want to risk this. He immediately fled, crossing the border to Malaysia.

After his escape, the other founders and their followers grew fearful. The government looked upon the Al-Mukmin boarding school as a place for extremism that was dangerous to the state. At that place, the followers not only learned about God, but also about politics. The state ideology came under scrutiny as much as religious ideology.

Meantime, the number of followers at the Ngruki site continued to grow. They came not only from the local community, but from around the country. In general, they were not aware of the controversy surrounding the school. They were interested in the principles taught there, but eventually they became uncomfortable after the authorities staged several raids.

The management at the boarding school changed on occasion. At various times it was chaired by Amir S.H. and Farid Ma'ruf. It had more than 5,000 students within its public and religious school system. Meanwhile, Abu Bakar Ba'syir disappeared and followed Abdullah Sungkar to Malaysia. After Hasan Basri passed away, the Ngruki school began to lose steam. Still, the activities at the boarding school continued.

The students at the Ngruki school spread to many places. Some of them established their own boarding schools, while others became teachers at existing schools. In the end, the formal activities at Ngruki ceased after its remaining students were arrested by the authorities. Not all were arrested, as some were able to escape. Some went to Lampung when they learned that there was a safe haven there. They reunited there in order to continue the Islamic study network.

In Lampung, the story of the Talangsari turmoil began. Initially, there were only a small number of students who joined Warsidi in his efforts to make an Islamic commune at Cihideung. When they regarded the situation as secure, they slowly brought their families to this site. There they joined with the members of the Lampung NII cell that had been confused after the infighting among its leadership. They also met the Jakarta group that had been looking around for a place to conduct their struggle.

Talangsari, therefore, became not just a center for the groups from Ngruki and Lampung. The Jakarta group that arrived included Nurhidayat, Ahmad Fauzi, Wahidin, and Sudarsono; they were very eager to monopolize their influence over the area.

The two former groups—from Ngruki and Lampung—were eventually influenced by the Jakarta group to create a base to carry out their struggle to realize the dream of the NII. This was never realized, because their ambitions caused a sharp reaction from the Talangsari III and Pakuan Aji communities, both of which supported the government authorities.

Such hopes, allegedly in the name of Islam, seemed appropriate for a country with a Muslim majority. A struggle in the name of Islam entails religious sacrifice. But such religious glory should never know the sharp end of a sword. The Prophet Muhammad established Madimatun Naby only through the use of good morals.***

14

BEHIND WARSIDI

WARSIDI was not alone, as there is no life that stands in isolation. Human beings need to be acknowledged. The more they are acknowledged, the stronger their existence. This was true of Warsidi. He became known because there were people around him that made him known. In truth, he was a small farmer and laborer that should have had little chance of being acknowledged by the general public.

As a group leader who taught Islam, he was held up by his followers as a spiritual leader rather than a teacher of Islam. According to statements by some of his followers, he lacked in many things, especially his ability to recite the Koran. Therefore, he never gave much emphasis to explaining the contents of the Koran and the teachings of the Prophet based on the study of books. He instead preferred to act as a symbol of unification rather than an intellectual with grand ideas. He did this in the hope of building an Islamic commune as a basis for struggle.

Who are the people who made Warsidi an important figure in the Cihideung area? What was their reaction toward Warsidi's actions when they came under question? The following people were those who were behind Warsidi.

Usman

❖ *There was a truly mysterious figure in Cihideung who successfully held up Warsidi as someone to idolize.*

Warsidi totally changed when Usman arrived at the commune. Previously, the commune at Cihideung was remote and unremarkable. Usman, an unknown figure, was able to influence the school and liven it up, not only as a place to recite the Koran, but also to curse and build up feelings of hatred for those with alternate views. These negative feelings were directed not only at the clerics and government, but also toward anybody not fully in line with their thinking. That is why he went as far as using words like infidel, tyrant, and the like.

Before joining Warsidi, Usman was born in Semarang on 13 September 1960. He had been a teacher at the Al Islam boarding school, about 1 kilometer north of Warsidi's commune. Al Islam was a small boarding school owned by Kiai Junaedi. Some people have said that Usman was very diplomatic and clever in attracting attention. However, he sometimes got into conflict with Kiai Junaedi, and Junaedi ultimately chased him off.

Though he was evicted from the boarding school, Usman was not alone. Ten followers from Al Islam moved with him to Warsidi's location in Talangsari. From that time forward, the commune grew more lively. His speech also grew more full of emotion. Unfortunately, the values he communicated touched on hate and hostility. Usman openly mocked Pancasila. He forbid his community from paying taxes or helping the village. He said that saluting the flag was the sign of an infidel, and to work for the state was illegal. Usman highly influenced Warsidi's way of thinking. He became the main tutor of the Cihideung commune.

For the commune, Usman was an intellectual and also an inventor. He was the one that created the Molotov cocktails they used. These were later used when Warsidi's group clashed with the masses and the authorities. These bombs spread terror in a number of places. These devices were made from empty bottles filled with sawdust and gas, then fitted with a fuse. They were effective in lighting fires against specific targets.

Usman is considered the one person most responsible after Warsidi for causing the unrest to take place. Before he went to Cihideung, Usman was suspected of being an anti-government activist. He spoke along these lines at several places, especially in Central Java and Yogyakarta.

In April 1985, he was sentenced by the Sleman-Yogyakarta District Court to one year in prison on the charge of slandering Soeharto in Temanggung, Sleman, Klaten, and Magelang. After serving that sentence, nothing further was heard about him until the turmoil at Talangsari.

Not many people know that it was through Usman that the Warsidi movement expanded its contacts outside of Lampung. Only after Usman came did other members begin to go from Jakarta and other places on Java to Warsidi's base camp at Cihideung.

Nurhidayat

❖ *Nurhidayat was once a customs and excise officer. He also practiced karate, but chose the life of an adventurer. His arrest was particularly dramatic.*

Nurhidayat was around 30 years old when the Cihideung unrest broke out. He was born in Jakarta on 26 March 1959, the second of four sons of Abdul Muthalib and Ning Suharni. His childhood was not a happy time. His father had financial trouble and sold all of their property. The little Nurhidayat followed his mother to Cilimus, Kuningan, Cirebon, West Java. His father, a retired soldier, stayed in Jakarta and made a living by opening a workshop in Tanah Abang.

Nurhidayat's skinny body was far from ideal. In poor health, he always looked like a weak child. But between his poor health, and the fact he was 17 years younger than his next elder sibling, he became a center of attention and was spoiled. He remained a highly dependent child. He also became shy and introverted. Among his schoolmates in junior and senior high school in Cirebon, he was often taunted and teased.

This spoiled child then took up karate to strengthen his spirit. He trained very seriously. After graduating from junior high school, he then followed his older brother, a mid-ranking police officer, back to Jakarta. His brother guided him as he became a skilled martial arts practitioner.

The world of karate started to give him some promise for the future. We won a competition for South Jakarta. From this, he was able to land a job as a customs and excise officer in 1980. He was in charge of the area of Tanjung Balai Karimun. Unfortunately, this proved a very lonely occupation and he soon took to drugs and alcohol. Intoxication and absenteeism became his new habits.

His performance dropped. He lost hope. His earlier poverty, the losses of his father's workshop: all of these began to pile up, making him frustrated and feeling that he was being treated unfairly.

Fortunately, Nurhidayat was able to release his frustrations by turning to religion. This became his new obsession. He met many religious teachers, and he attended many Islamic study classes. He concluded that Islamic justice and law needed to be upheld. Eventually, he left his job as a customs officer and state employee. He then chose a career as a businessman. He saw this as more respectful than being a state employee because he now regarded the latter as a job for infidels.

Nurhidayat and his friends then established their own Islamic study group. A number of youths, including Sudarsono and Fauzi, also joined him and supported one another. In their broader organizational structure, Nurhidayat was placed in charge of the contingent codenamed 'Ali.' This contingent was one of the groups that was supposed to move to Cihideung.

This study group was very focused on building up their militant cadres. They were especially intent on hating the New Order government. One of their phases of training involved fasting for 40 days, during which time they reciting verses intensively and performed group prayers in the middle of the night. Those who passed this phase then went to Lampung to join Warsidi to build the base at Cihideung.

After the Talangsari unrest broke out, Nurhidayat was arrested by the authorities at Cipinang Melayu in East Jakarta at the end of February 1989. During that time, he and his friends were hiding in Haji Armad's rented house. Nurhidayat tried to escape through the roof. The authorities were not fooled, and they arrested him on the roof. He told the arresting officer that his name was 'Abdullah,' but he later revealed that his true name was Nurhidayat.

From the rented house, the officers seized a number of poisoned arrows and a bow. They also found several Molotov cocktails, chemical substances, and several maps covering a number of regions.

Sudarsono

❖ *Sudarsono's name is the one most often mentioned when people talk about Talangsari and Warsidi.*

Though he rarely stayed at Talangsari, this well-built man had an important role in Warsidi's life struggle. He was the one that inspired the poisoned arrows, and helped control the commune activities in Talangsari, Lampung.

Sudarsono was born in Belawan, Deli Serdang, North Sumatra, on 21 April 1963. He father was a sergeant major in the army. Though born in Sumatra, he preferred to consider himself a native of East Java.

He first became involved in organized religious activity when he joined the Indonesian Mosque Communications Board at the Al Falah mosque in Suarabaya. After passing senior high school, he moved to Jakarta in 1983, then continued his studies at the As Syafi'iyah Business School and the Open University. He then ceased his studies for various reasons. After the As Syafi'iyah Business Schooll and the As Syafi'iyah Islamic University merged, he became active in the Development Study Board, a non-government organization led by Adi Sasono.

He was also active in a campus Islamic study group called Farmy (an abbreviation for the Inter Islamic Student Forum). In this group, he met Nurhidayat, Fauzi, and several others; together they later established their own group in Jakarta that was subsequently linked to Warsidi's activities in Talangsari. This group also came up with the idea of establishing an Islamic commune as a base for struggling to establish NII in Indonesia.

Sudarsono chose Talangsari as the center for this activity because of its strategic location and its accessibility from all directions, including Jakarta. In addition, Warsidi was seen as somebody with potential. He was seen as someone who could realize the goal of an Islamic commune. For Darsono, the Talangsari turmoil saddened him because it ruined his hopes. It also made Darsono a fugitive. He moved from one place to another to escape the pursuing authorities. Eventually, he was arrested after his friend, Marfaid Harapan, betrayed him and reported him to the authorities.

Coincidentally, some of his other friends were arrested at nearly the same time. Sukardi was shot in the leg. Heriyanto, Ridwan, Maulana, Dede Syaiffudin, and Abdullah Fatah Qosim were also arrested.

Ahmad Fauzi Isnan

❖ *His story is unique. Born into a military family, he never showed any trace of respect for the military during his entire life. He even tried to establish a force to confront the military. What went wrong?*

Fauzi was just 22 years old when the Cihideung turmoil took place. However, he had an important role in Warsidi's group. Together with Nurhidayat, Sudarsono, and Wahidin, they were among those that thought up the idea of making an Islamic commune at Cihideung that would oppose the government. Fauzi actually comes from a family that had long lived in Lampung. He spent his youth in a military complex, where his father was a member of the army. The third of five children, he grew up in the *Black Garuda* complex in Lampung.

During his childhood, Fauzi spent time learning about Islam, including how to recite the Koran and how to write Arabic. This is because his family was very focused on religion. His parents supported him in his studies, and his siblings were also very involved in religion. After graduating from elementary school in 1982, he went to senior high school in Tanjung Karang. However, he dropped out in his second year.

Fauzi then moved to the Tambak Beras boarding school in Jombang, East Java and graduated from

Islamic senior high school. After that he went to Jakarta and was accepted into the Central Bureau of Statistics. While working at the bureau, he was sent to the Statistical Academy, which he passed in 1988. However, after graduating from this academy, he chose not to return to his office. Instead he chose to attend an Islamic study group. While there, he met Sudarsono and Nurhidayat. During a meeting at Ciloto, West Java in March 1988, they established an organization to establish the NII in Talangsari, Lampung. This group briefly disbanded, but later came together under Wahidin's influence in Condet, East Jakarta.

After Darsono introduced himself to Warsidi, it is said that Fauzi and Nurhidayat tricked dozens of people into going to Lampung. These people later became the victims of the Talangsari turmoil that shook the world in 1989.

Today, Fauzi has his own version of what took place during the Cihideung upheaval. According to him, the Talangsari incident was started when an Islamic study group tried to establish an Islamic commune after having been scattered. Warsidi offered a piece of land in Cihideung as the location for the commune. Around December 1988, study groups from Solo, Bandung, and Jakarta converged to join Warsidi in Cihideung.

Together, these groups totaled more than 100 people, says Fauzi, which caused the authorities to get suspicious. On 6 Feburary 1989, the commander of the military sub-district, Soetiman, drove with a jeep and eight motorbikes to Warsidi's commune. Suspecting that they would come under attack, Warsidi struck with arrows. Soetiman was killed in the incident.

That night, the army surrounded the commune. A battle broke out after sunrise, while a second incident at Sidorejo against the village chief, Arifin Santoso, was carried out according to Warsidi's instruction. Regarding the death of Private Budi, Fauzi says that the officer was killed by one of Warsidi's followers outside of Cihideung while they were together riding in a rented vehicle. The killing took place because Warsidi's members hated the army; when they saw Private Budi wearing a military uniform, they immediately killed him.

Fauzi is basing these statements on what was reported in the news. He was actually in Jakarta when the incident took place. According to Darsono, his comrade Fauzi did not have much first-hand knowledge about Cihideung or Talangsari. Darsono said that Fauzi went there only once. Fauzi claimed to the author that he went to Talangsari twice.

Regarding what was said by Fauzi, there is still controversy because he was not there himself. According to several of his friends, he has a very unique character. Psychologically, he is unstable both in his thinking and his actions. In particular, he betrayed and deceived his own associates. His relationships with his friends is clearly not harmonious.

In fact, after he was released from prison in 1999, Fauzi initiated the process of reconciliation as a way of resolving the case. But then he backtracked on this and set up a 'Committee for the Victims of Military Violence' in Lampung, which has constantly tried to reopen the case. It was only resolved because of the efforts of Hendropriyono.

All of which was regarded as a betrayal by those that opted for reconciliation. According to his friends, both sides in the dispute have closed the case and have sought reconciliation.

Riyanto

❖ *In the eyes of Warsidi, there were two people who were appropriate to be chosen as a commander. One of them was Riyanto. This man, together with Fadhillah (alias Sugito), was entrusted by Warsidi to carry out the terror campaign in Lampung eleven years ago.*

At first glance, one would not believe that Riyanto, 48, could have a hot temper. But this temper has been seen by many people as something which was horrible. In Lampung eleven years ago, when the Wardidi turmoil broke out, one of the main players was Riyanto. Together with Fadhillah, Riyanto successfully led his members in creating the Lampung turmoil in 1989.

Riyanto came to know of Warsidi from his friend, Aminuddin, who said that there was a place in Lampung that was going to be established as a base for establishing NII. Riyanto was interested in this story, but wanted to see it for himself.

He immediately went to Lampung to verify the tale. He was able to confirm that there was a group of people with these ideals. Riyanto then decided to immediately join Warsidi's struggle. He joined the group led by Alex, and had his wife and three children join him from Tanjung Priok.

Riyanto was prepared to meet his destiny with people he did not really know, including Warsidi. He also had to meet his destiny after five of Warsidi's members were arrested and Warsidi ordered Riyanto to gain their release from the authorities. Together with Fadhillah and some other followers, he became a killer and a person who stirred up trouble for many people.

After being released from Nusakambangan prison, people still did not know much about Riyanto's activities. However, many people came to pester him about the Talangsari case. For example, Fauzi Isnan claimed that the persons who were released from prison were given money, a house, land, and even cows as a way of silencing them. After Riyanto was accused of this, he wrote a rebuttal to the press. In his letter, he exposed Fauzi's low morals.

Riyanto's Rebuttal

Riyanto's published his rebuttal in *Panji Masyarakat* magazine on 3 May 2000. He said that it was not true that those who committed murder in Talangsari received money, a house, land, and even cows as a way of silencing them, even though Fauzi Isnan had made this claim in the media.

According to Riyanto, it was actually Fauzi who benefited the most from the reconciliation arranged by Hendropriyono in 1998. Fauzi asked that a Kijang car be provided to the Bunaya Foundation for those who were released. However, the car was misused and later sold by Fauzi.

Riyanto admitted that several of those who were convicted of the Talangsari murders were compensated by Hendropriyono, but this was limited to those who had just been released from prison. Fauzi, by contrast, had profited much more.

Riyanto stated that if Fauzi does not stop slandering and making trouble, Fauzi would find himself in big trouble.

Clarification by the former Commander of Warsidi's rebel force

*(3 May 2000 edition of **Panji Masyarakat**, pp. 10-11)*

Referring to the news release of 18 April 2000, page 8, titled 'Trying to Gag the Talangsari Murders,' I, as one of the former prisoners of the Talangsari case, object to the contents of this item which has originated from Mr. Fauzi Isnan. It is not true that those involved with the Talangsari case have been persuaded not to bring up the case, and have been paid off in the form of cash, houses land, and cows.

Our efforts, such as the demonstration in front of the National Human Rights Commission, are to halt the steps taken by Mr. Fauzi Isnan, who intends to reopen the Talangsari case. Previously, Fauzi and his friends were the ones that proposed the reconciliation process in 1998.

As far as we know, Mr. Fauzi Isnan and his friends at that time (1998) did much in the name of the Talangsari case and earned much financial benefit from the reconciliation process. Fauzi Isnan even made his own personal use of a Kijang car donated by Hendropriyono, which was supposed to be used by the Bunaya Foundation for the business affairs of all ex-Talangsari prisoners. Instead, he controlled the car and it eventually disappeared.

To those that were convicted of the Talangsari murders, Hendropriyono actually gave a Lebaran bonus in the form of cash amounting to millions of rupiah for those that were recently released from prison and did not yet have a source of income. Thus, it was not given to all of those convicted in the case. Mr. Fauzi actually received a much larger Lebaran bonus than some of the other released prisoners.

In addition, a donation of four cows was to be provided jointly to all of the prisoners who came from Solo, Central Java, but not for their private interests. Thus far, however, the four cows have been difficult to find, and have offered no benefits to those from Solo.

Our objective is to remind Mr. Fauzi Isnan, who is now on probation, not to do anything wrong. He has already received sufficient financial and material benefits from Hendropriyono by exploiting the name of the Talangsari case. We fear that if Hendropriyono brings the case of the misused Kijang to court, Mr. Fauzi could one again land in prison.

Riyanto, former commander of Warsidi's rebel force.

Zamzuri

❖ *Zamzuri had an important indirect role in Warsidi's struggle. This rich man from Sidoredjo was not just honored, but also beloved by those who struggled in their hope of creating the NII in Lampung.*

The distance between Zamzuri's house in Sideredjo and Warsidi's commune in Cihideung was far, about 30 kilometers. Zamzuri lived in downtown Sidoredjo, while Warsidi lived in the forest of Cihideung. It was in Zamzuri's house that the Cihideung activists frequently stopped. As a result, Zamzur's house was never empty of visitors, making the neighbors suspicious and jealous—especially the authorities.

If there had not been for the murder of some officials and civilians in Sidoredjo, Zamzuri's name would not be remembered in dark terms by this pepper town. The turmoil at the foot of Balak Mountain showed the tension between the authorities and Warsidi's group, the latter of which had declared war on the government. This turmoil had a long impact and caused great misfortune, not only to Zamzuri, but also to ordinary citizens.

The story began with suspicions among the authorities that something was wrong in Zamzuri's house. When they went to investigate, a person came running out toward the officials. The police fired a warning shot, but the person tried to grab the weapon; he was eventually shot dead.

Knowing that one of their members was dead, Zamzuri and his friends got angry. Emerging from the house, they gave chase to Dargo, the police officer who shot their comrade. In what became known as the Balak Mountain Incident, they eventually killed Dargo (the Gunung Balak sector commander), Santoso Arifin (the village head of Sidoredjo), and Giono (a teacher at the Muhammadiyah Junior High School). Injured, too, were several members of Warsidi's group. Zamzuri was later brought to court and imprisoned in Nusakambangan for more than ten years before being released as a result of the reconciliation process.

Today, this man who was born in Gunugn Kudul in Yogyakarta in 1942 and was seen as a success in the Gunung Balak area of Lampung, is enjoying his golden years in Sidoredjo. While in prison, he learned to get a more grounded spiritual life. The past is past. He has vowed not to make any mistakes during his second chance at life.

To the author, he admitted that he must learn more about life. According to him, there is not such thing as being useless in the eyes of God. He realized that all of the suffering that took place was God's intention and it was best for him as a human being.

As a result, when he heard that several people wanted to file charges against the authorities because they saw the officials as guilty, Zamzuri chose not to be involved.

In fact, he said that those looking to prosecute the authorities are the ones that should be prosecuted. The authorities were only doing their duty, something that was their responsibility.

For Zamzuri, the truth will come out. He will always come together with his people who love peace.***

15

RECONCILIATION AS AN ALTERNATE SOLUTION

EVERYONE hopes for peace. All of God's creation needs merciful peace. Only in a peaceful setting can one travel from one place to another. It is not just individuals or groups that hope for peace: entire nations strive for it. All methods are used for reaching peace.

When there is a dispute or quarrel, Islam teaches that peace can be reached through reconciliation. Peace through reconciliation was even used by God's prophets as a way of solving problems. In this country, reconciliation seems to be popular as a theory taught by preachers of Islam. But it is only popular to a limited audience in Islamic schools and universities. For the rest, the concept of reconciliation is seen as mere words in religious literature that is read only when necessary.

For a country that has been hard hit by disputes, where we have grown bored of hearing about fights within our communities, we have been surprised to hear about parties willing to arrive at peaceful reconciliation. Though reconciliation might be the hope of many, few have tried to understand the concept.

The concept of reconciliation became a reality for the group in Lampung in 1998. This focused on the persons that had been responsible for the Talangsari turmoil in 1989. By that time, one of the former members of Warsidi's group, Fauzi Isnan, proposed reconciliation along with some of his friends to Hendropriyono, the former chief of the *Black Garuda* military region in Lampung when the conflict took place. Hendro welcomed Fauzi's concept after having had the meaning of reconciliation explained to him. A.M. Hendropriyono was then named as the facilitator for arranging the reconciliation.

Hendropriyono's enthusiasm for reconciliation was welcomed by A.M. Fatwa, who at the time was responsible for rehabilitating two of the figures in the Lampung incident, Fauzi and Nurhidayat. Through A.M. Fatwa, a meeting was held between Hendropriyono and fourteen former members of Warsidi's group. This meeting was held without incident and touched on various matters. According to Yani Wahid, the person who was the inspiration behind writing this book, the meeting of the two parties had a positive atmosphere as if there had been no previous conflict between them.

'We were performing our destiny. We very much regret the Talangsari incident. How can we draw lessons from this unintended event of the past? We could do something which benefits the present.' This was how Hendropriyono opened the discussion after offering some introductory remarks. Those from the Talangsari case that were in attendance included Sudarsono, Fauzi Isnan, Sukardi, Dede Saifudin, and Maulana Latif.

The reconciliation, they agreed, would be a small chapter for a country that was otherwise in total disarray. Never before had a senior official been willing to meet with persons who had been categorized as a militant group. Thus, what Hendropriyono did was a unique event. He was a general and a minister, but he was willing to associate himself with opponents and victims in a voluntary reconciliation.

The main agenda of the reconciliation talks was to release those in prison. Initially, Hendropriyono was able to release just three prisoners. But then Darsono said that it would be better to have none released rather than just three. Darsono demanded that 15 of his friends confined to Nusakambangan prison be set free. The end result of the reconciliation was that all of the Lampung prisoners were able to breathe the fresh air of freedom.

The light of peace illuminated their hearts. This included those from Warsidi's group, the Way Jepara community, and the authorities represented by

A.M. Hendropriyono. On that day, they swore that they would ignore the dark past and step toward a better future. They were the warriors who had implemented the Islamic principle of reconciliation.

The Moral Basis of Reconciliation

Reconciliation has a strong moral basis. The word appears frequently in the Holy Koran. It literally means reconciliation, or improvement. The principle of reconciliation generally means a comprehensive improvement covering faith, worship, morals, the economy, politics, and other facets.

The principle focuses on improving what has been made good. It also refers to recovering things that have been ruined, such as social relationships. These relationships could have been ruined by conflicts, hostility, disputes, blasphemy, greed, and other reasons.

In order to realize reconciliation, there must be a certain psychological condition—namely, a proper moral foundation that covers all of the individuals involved, as well as emotional control, generosity, and a lack of stubbornness.

There can be no reconciliation if either party is still tempted by an unenlightened spirit or unenlightened action: such dark characteristics do not enable the individual to distinguish between good and bad. For example, if they do not repent about their violent ways, or turn a deaf ear to good, or tear apart the truth and are blind to realities.

In the eyes of the Koran, dark desires are the cause of eternal hostility and misery, and have caused countless disasters in the history of human civilization.

When there was a horrifying conflict in which all sides almost killed each other off in Madinah, God's Prophet quickly acted to put an end to this by saying:

'Ye faithful that have ignored God, you have been tempted by unenlightened spirits. Remember I am here between you. Remember that God has led us to Islam, to glorify you, to draw you away from unenlightened atheism, and bring you together in friendship.'

Thus, the Prophet of God brought about reconciliation by making them realize they were tempted by the devil.

In addition, the Prophet of God applied the concept of reconciliation when there was bloodshed. The Prophet tried to stop ethnic ignorance and rivalry. For example, in the eighth year, an armed force led by Khalid bin Walid was provoked and started killing members of the Banu Jadhimah ethnic group. The Prophet brought about reconciliation by giving Ali bin Abu Thalib the order, 'As soon as possible go to them, observe this strictly, and stop your unenlightened ways!' Ali quickly went to the designated place, and gave much monetary compensation for lost property and casualties.

When the Prophet referred to unenlightened ways, he was referring to the inability to control oneself from anger, such as was the case with Khalid and his troops.

In both of the above cases, reconciliation was applied during the era of the Prophet. Through reconciliation, the Prophet created brotherhood, peace, and harmony, and ended conflict and hostility. In actuality, reconciliation is a practical way of solving political fragmentation within a community. The Prophet of God also applied the principle of amnesty, such as when he offered amnesty to the Mecca community in order to bring an end to conflict and hostility.

In this era of reform, we, the largest community in Indonesia, would appear to be lost if Islam seems to teach its believers only to prosecute and punish, rather than forgive in order to face the future. We should bear in mind the Prophet of God's policy when he was chased and stoned by the Thaif community. Or the lesson when the Prophet restored public unity after liberating Mecca and not shaming Abu Sofyan, who had been well known as the Prophet's enemy for almost twenty years. There are many other instances when the Prophet applied reconciliation to restore the dignity of all parties and bring out peace—this applied to both individual dignity and institutional dignity.

As a concept, reconciliation will always appeal to all parties in a community who intend to improve the situation and improve broken ties due to conflicts or disputes.

Among those who speak about human rights and enforcing democracy, it is often possible to find groups who intend to file charges about past cases with human rights tribunals.

But if the case is very complex, this might not be effective because it could cause new conflicts to be justified by formal institutions. There are many examples, in fact, where courts have caused legal troubles that they could not correct. Therefore, the choice to apply the concept of reconciliation as a religious alternative can be seen as appropriate in closing episodes of past political shortcomings that undercut solidarity and harmony.

In applying this concept, the main value is in restoring relationships that will reunify a community that was beset by conflict. This is not a matter for the courts to recover dignity and respect, whether it be the honor of individuals, institutions, or community leaders. Given the current condition of the Indonesian community at large, reconciliation is urgently needed to help in the recovery of domestic relations and friendships, and as a way of rectifying old cases seen to be the result of earlier institutional repression.

In the context of Islamic morals, the parties involved should endeavor to heal each other and erect models of patience, love, and affection.***

16

THE RESPONSE TO RECONCILIATION

PROLONGED social and political conflict can cause the dignity of the state and nation to wither. After the New Order, all elements of the community hoped that conflict among the political elite and between communities could be immediately brought to an end.

Islam, as the religion followed by the majority of Indonesians, offers specific insights into conflict-resolution while restoring honor and dignity. One of the moral concepts taught by Islam is to have reconciliation between conflicting parties. This strengthens friendships through forgiveness and joint deliberation on solutions. This concept was the moral basis for the reconciliation among the parties in the Lampung case. Their intention should be lauded since it intended to not only solve the conflict, but also contribute to the creation of a smooth and harmonious social climate in a community that had experienced an upheaval.

Spreading the reconciliation concept is not an easy thing to do, especially given that the desire to enforce human rights and prosecute abuses is seen as an important process. It might also be the case that part of the community does not agree with forgiving a community member. Not forgiving is an individual right. Moreover, it is the obligation of the state to prosecute. The law must be upheld if there is a violation.

For such people, the legal approach is considered of primary importance. But Arifin, the former political prisoner from the Talangsari case, believes differently. Arifin believes that the most important thing is to release his friends who are still imprisoned, and to assist them in getting jobs and compensating the families of victims. Regarding reconciliation, he said, 'We have directly met Bpk. Hendro. We have forgiven each other. We chose a solution from Islamic law, reconciliation, rather than make a counter-case, especially since revenge is forbidden by Islam.'

Arifin acknowledges he has dark memories of Talangsari. His wife and children were killed in the incident. 'If we follow an unenlightened path, our desire is to rebel. But I am sure that even until the end of the world, justice and law enforcement will never be achieved as long as we apply secular laws.' (*Lampung Pos*, 5 September 1989)

The human rights issues that have recently surfaced are indeed difficult to resolve, and it will probably not be appropriate to judge past issues and violations that have political overtones. The Lampung case is an example of a past issue that has become an easy target for human rights activists. But who will benefit from reopening the issue? Are interest groups involved? The parties that were directly involved in the Talangsari incident decided to apply reconciliation, not the legal process. But NGOs have criticized reconciliation. Why have they done this? Why have they recently started to defend Warsidi and his case? Have they previously shown an interest in the Warsidi group, especially the widows, those that lost their jobs, and those that were imprisoned? Why are they only now pushing this case as if it were very important to them? All of these questions have been asked by Sudarsono.

According to Sudarsono, it is useless to bring up the past if it gives no benefit to the community or brings welfare to victims. He is irate over the way certain NGOs look for international funding to disturb Indonesia in the name of human rights. Sudarsono and other political prisoners hope that the generous attitude taken by people like Hendropriyono in the Lampung case, along with economic assistance, can be a model for other top leaders to ensure that other political victims are not used by certain interest groups without benefiting victims and their families. (*Republika*, 10 September 1998).

Many people have questioned who actually benefits by those who claim to be delving into human rights issues. The following is a more detailed explanation by the former detainees in the Warsidi case regarding reconciliation and public opinion.***

A Statement of the Victims from the Lampung Incident

Signed by **Fauzi Isnan**, one of those who pushed for reconciliation
Dated 13 August 1998

We do not intend to involve ourselves in a political struggle among political powers who act in the name of reform by using political events of the Soeharto era as a vehicle for the interests of individuals or certain political groups.

We request the Habibie government to immediately release all political prisoners without conditions.

This is especially true for the Lampung case, which has been resolved through a meeting between the concerned parties. We do not want to involve other parties that wish to exploit or politicize the case.

NOTES

1. Fauzi Isnan's attitude has changed since February 2000 following a conflict with Sudarsono concerning the misuse of vehicles belonging to the Bunaya Foundation.
2. Sudarsono claims that his friend, Fauzi, misused foundation property and must be held accountable under the law.

Sudarsono's Views

Sent to various newspapers
3 November 1998

As part of the Warsidi community, we have thought deeply about a way of settling the issue according to the Holy Koran. Namely, we used reconciliation, not a legal approach or counter-charges as suggested by some NGOs which we believe had political aims to play off the Islamic community and the military against each other.

Our findings in the field found that many people who used to criticize the Islamic cause by calling it rightwing extremism or separatism have suddenly recast themselves as helpers of God who intend to prosecute our case according to secular law. They have used flawed logic to see the issue with only their interests in mind.

We, the former detainees in the Lampung case, have jointly chosen to pursue reconciliation. Through reconciliation, we hope that the Lampung case will be spared from political exploitation from certain parties who are looking for personal profit.

As a Muslim, Hendropriyono, the former *Black Garuda* military region commander, is more of a gentleman than others who have never cared for their victims. We regard Hendropriyono's private approach as a model moral step that shows him to be an example of a person who applies his religion to the values of humanity.

We realize that reconciliation will not be a politically popular step given that human rights issues are constantly being spotlighted. However, we should not be blind to religious wisdom. We have chosen religious wisdom in order to avoid the evil of those prepared to use slander and prosecution.

"In uriidu illal-ishlal mastatho 'tu"

A PUBLIC RESPONSE

Saiful Abas
Tanah Abang, Jakarta

Reconciliation is more Islamic

Let us stop the mudslinging among us, especially those intent on humiliating another's dignity. Given the current unhealthy condition of the country, let us spare some space in our hearts to recover our unity. Let us stop the hatred and revenge. Let's not waste time to revel in another person's disgrace, and let's especially not intentionally look for the chance to ruin another person's dignity.

I was very apprehensive when I read the reader's response in which he complained about the intention to bring about reconciliation between Hendropriyono and the former prisoners. Why should this be criticized? I think they have fundamental reasons for mutual forgiveness.

I support their way of peaceful settlement because it has a more Islamic flavor.

(as printed in the 20 November 1998 issue of ***Suara Mimbar***)

H. Firdaus
Bekasi

Let us use the model of the Prophet of God

In many examples in history, the Prophet of God gives priority to the use of reconciliation for bringing back love and affection in relationships. He never brings up past political wounds, but closes all conflicts in order to reflect the glory of Islamic morals. In the liberation of Mecca, all of the people who were liberated were spared from shame.

Even Abu Sofyan, who was his enemy for almost twenty years, did not have his dignity come under attack. The Prophet of God still honored and respected his dignity as a political leader during the liberation of Mecca.

Therefore, let us not make past political cases a hindrance for bringing about good relations. Let us model ourselves on the Prophet's morals as was stated in the Koran: Don't make God a hindrance since you have taken an oath in His name to act with good conduct and devotion to make reconciliation! (Al-Baqarah, 224)

For my friends who have just been released from prison, I want to remind you that our past leaders—M. Natsir, Hamka, Roem, and Prawoto—never slandered Sukarno after he released them from prison!

(as printed in the 15 November 1998 issue of ***Media Indonesia***)

Ismail Zuklarnain

Head of the National Reconciliation Support Committee in Lampung.

The Necessity of Seeking a Wise Settlement

In the effort to look into political cases and human rights abuses, we should seek wise settlements. In this way, we hope that all matters can be settled without disturbing the government and thereby allowing the authorities to overcome the current crisis.

The noise of demonstrators and their sporadic protests can cause disorder, leading the country to fall further into political and economic crisis. Therefore, the National Reconciliation Support Committee believes that the effort to settle past cases must be aimed at bringing about national unity to prevent instability through disintegration.

(***Harian Pagi Tamtama*,**
Lampung, 26 September 1998)

Victims Regard the Talangsari Case as Over

The victims of the Talangsari case in Way Jepara, Central Lampung, also known as the Warsidi rebel group, stated that they believed the case was over since reconciling with Lieutenant General Hendropriyono, the former *Black Garuda* military region commander.

'We regard the case as over,' was the conclusion reached at a one-day seminar that aimed to look for the settlement of political cases and human rights violations in Lampung. The seminar was held at the Taman Budaya building in Lampung.

The settlement through reconciliation began 14 days after President Soeharto's resignation. The meetings resulted in three important agreements. First, there was amnesty for all those still imprisoned ; those sentenced to life in prison will have their cases reviewed for clemency. Second, there will be an economic assistance effort to assist the Lampung victims, including those from Warsidi's group, the local community, and the authorities. Third, there will be social rehabilitation programs for the victims and their families.

(***Lampung Pos***, 27 September 1998)

LEGISLATIVE ASSEMBLY FOR EAST LAMPUNG DISTRICT

Address: Jalan Ir. Soekarno-Sukadana Telephone: 42578–42586

DECREE
OF THE LEGISLATIVE ASSEMBLY
OF EAST LAMPUNG DISTRICT

Number 170/3/2/XII/SK/DPRD-LTM/2000

ON

THE TALANGSARI, WAY JEPARA CASE
EAST LAMPUNG DISTRICT

With God's Blessing

The East Lampung Legislative Assembly considers:

a. That the incident at Talangsari hamlet, Way Jepara sub-district, East Lampung on 6–7 February 1989 is over based on positive legal processes that prevail in Indonesia.

b. That recently, a small number of persons outside of the East Lampung district have attempted to reopen the Talangsari case.

c. That according to statements made by the persons who instigated the Talangsari case, their families, and the victims and their families from the communities of Rajabasa Lama village, Labuahan Ratu Induk village, and Labuhan Ratu IV village in Way Jepara sub-district, East Lampung, to the East Lampung district Legislative Assembly on 14 July 2000, they intend not to reopen the Talangsari case for the sake of those killed in the incident as well as for the public peace in Talangsari hamlet in particular, and the East Lampung district community in general.

d. That in observance of points b and c, as well as the opinions expressed by the community regarding the Talangsari case, the East Lampung district Legislative Assembly established a special team to look into the Talangsari case based on the assembly's decision #170/12/VIII/SK/Pimp.DPRD-LTM/2000 dated 7 August 2000.

e. That the result of field observations of the Talangsari special team showed that the belief, which had been politicized by certain persons, that there had been assassinations by the security authorities was not true and contradicted the facts.

f. That the Talangsari case was caused by the establishment of an Islamic commune in the Cihideung area of Talangsari III hamlet by Wasidi, and this Islamic group was provoked by four groups in order to make them agitated to the point of disturbing the public order to achieve their goals.

In view of:

1. Law #14/1964 on the establishment of Lampung province (State Gazette of the Republic of Indonesia, #95/1964, and Supplementary State Gazette #2688)
2. Law #12/1999 on the establishment of Way Kanan district, East Lampung district, and Metro Municipality (State Gazette of the Republic of Indonesia, #46/1999, and Supplementary State Gazette #3825)
3. Law #22/1999 on Regional Governments (State Gazette of the Republic of Indonesia, #60/1999, and Supplementary State Gazette 3839)
4. Law #4/1999 on the structure and position of the MPR, DPR, and DPRD (State Gazette of the Republic of Indonesia, #24/1999, and Supplementary State Gazette #3811)

5. Decision of the Lampung Governor #G/274/B.III/HK/1999 dated 16 August 1999 on the official announcement of membership of the East Lampung district Legislative Assembly and the Decision of Lampung Governor G/274/B.III/HK/1999 dated ...1999 on the official announcement of the supplemental membership of the East Lampung district Legislative Assembly and Decision of Lampung Governor G/322/B.III/HK/1999 dated 17 September 1999 on the official announcement of the management of the East Lampung district Legislative Assembly.
6. Decision of the management of the East Lampung district Legislative Assembly #170/12/VIII/SK/PIM.DPRD-LTM/2000 dated 7 August 2000 on Personnel Structure of the membership of a special committee on the Talangsari case.

Observing:

a. The results of the meeting of the East Lampung district Legislative Assembly dated 22 November 2000;
b. The Aspirations and the contributions of the perpetrators, their families, the victims, and the victim's families killed in the upheaval specifically in Talangsari, Way Jepara sub-district and Sidorejo village in Sekampung Udik sub-district, and in East Lampung in general;
c. The report of the Talangsari special committee;
d. The Final conclusion of the East Lampung district Legislative Assembly.

IT HAS BEEN DECIDED TO PROMULGATE

THE DECISION OF THE EAST LAMPUNG DISTRICT LEGISLATIVE ASSEMBLY ON THE TALANGSARI CASE IN WAY JEPARA SUB-DISTRICT IN EAST LAMPUNG

First,

For the achievement of peace and stability in East Lampung district, the community refuses to reopen the 1989 Talangsari case and considers the case closed.

Second,

That a settlement has been achieved by almost all involved (the perpetrators, their families, the victims of both parties, and the families of the victims of both parties). This applies to the community of Rajabasa Lama village, Way Jepara sub-district, and Sidorejo village, Sekampung Udik sub-district in particular, and East Lampung district in general. They have used reconciliation in accordance with Islamic precepts, to which they are devoted.

Third,

To request competent officers from either the central or regional government, as well as community figures and the public, not to reopen the Talangsari case, but rather to start economic development of East Lampung district to achieve material and non-material prosperity.

Fourth,

This decision is effective as of this date; in the event of mistakes, they will be rectified immediately.

Promulgated in Sukadana
On 10 December 2006
DEWAN PERWAKILAN RAKYAT DAERAH
KABUPATEN LAMPUNG TIMUR
KETUA,

ISMAIL SANJAYA

17

THOSE THAT WERE RELEASED

WHAT is the meaning of prison? It refers to confining a man. Their fate is determined for them. They are given orders. It is unimaginable. Those who used to freely exercise their choices and could decide wherever they wanted to go, can no longer do so. They can not eat or drink what they want to. They can not associate with their children, their wives, and their loved ones.

They are limited by regulations enforced by the wardens, people who can be polite on one occasion but very angry at another. The wardens can be very generous in their words—almost like a priest—but they can shoot you with a bullet if you try to escape. This can make one sink into mental shock: depression, hysteria, anxiety, and utter powerlessness for all but those with a strong mental will. How do they spend their sentence of many years, or even life sentences?

No one wishes to be imprisoned, especially at Nusakambangan prison. This includes those that were involved in the Talangsari turmoil in Way Jepara, Central Lampung, like Dede Saefudin, Sukardi, and Maulana Latif. They never wanted to be imprisoned, nor did their other friends at Nusakambangan.

When they first attended their reconciliation meeting with former transmigration minister A.M. Hendropriyono, their initial request was to get the release of their friends from Nusakambangan. Previously, Hendro would only release a few of those who had been accused of political crimes. He did not include those Lampung prisoners who had been charged with murder and killing. However, after the request was put forward and reconciliation was supported by Mr. Fauzi, Mr. Hendro eventually agreed and requested the data on those still in prison. According to Dede Saefudin in an interview with the author, Hendro processed the release in his capacity as a minister. According to Dede, it was agreed one night that a number of people would go to Nusakambangan the next morning to bring news of the reconciliation as well as to start compiling data on the Lampung prisoners who had not yet been released. He said that he thought the person in charge of compiling the data and relaying it to Mr. Hendro was Mr. Maulana Latif.

The desire to immediately release the political prisoners gained momentum, as it became a top issue on the reform agenda. It was not just political prisoners that appealed for release, but other members of the community such as Islamic leaders and members of Islamic mass organizations. But these appeals would have been meaningless unless there had been a senior official who wanted to process the proposals.

The process of gaining their release was held by those with legal power, and was in fact not an easy thing to do. There needed to be a party to make an official request, then it had to be discussed by several departments to confirm whether or not the release was possible and was justified by prevailing laws and regulations.

By that time, Attorney General H.A. Muhammad Galib S.H. indicated that the amnesty was possible provided that:

1. The person had not been in prison more than ten years.
2. They needed to give a statement of loyalty to the unity of the Republic of Indonesia.
3. They promised not to conduct any further activities that would threaten the unity of the state.

The euphoria of reform continued. Still, the political prisoners were not to be automatically released, not even on the 17 August 1998 national day. Feeling responsible after having agreed to reconciliation, Minister of Transmigration A.M. Hendropriyono was finally able to deliver his promise.

Through letter R-028/Mentras/08/1998 dated 21 August 1998, the Minister of Transmigration and Resettlement wrote to the President of the Republic of

Indonesia requesting that the process of releasing the political prisoners from the Lampung case be accelerated. Not relying only on this letter, he directly lobbied Attorney General A.M. Ghalib, Minister of Justice Muladi, Minister of Defense and Security Wiranto, and Supreme Court judge Sarwata. As a result, the Attorney General produced letter R-196/A/D.9/1998 dated 23 September 1998 advising the president to fulfill the request of the Minister of Transmigration with regard to the amnesty. A month later, the Minister of State, Akbar Tanjung, sent letter R-311/M. Sesneg/10/1998 dated 26 October 1998 to the Coordinating Minister for Defense and Security, the Minister of Justice, and the Minister for Defense and Security notifying them about the president's guidance on the proposal for rehabilitating the political prisoners of the Lampung case. Fauzi and his friends were to be assisted in this process.

This proved that, even though it was the era of reform, the release of Islamic political prisoners was not as easy as many had imagined. The bureaucracy was extremely meticulous, with requests going from the top to bottom and then back to the top again, before being signed by the President of the Republic of Indonesia.

In the process of releasing several prisoners from the Lampung case, President Bacharuddin Jusuf Habibie signed the decision for clemency after passing through a strict process. This was especially true because the Law on Subversion had not yet been revoked at that time. Eventually, however, with Presidential Decree 101/

10/1998 dated 31 December 1999, the President fulfill the clemency of the prisoners of the Lampung case that had been pushed by the Minister of Transmigration.

Those who were released:

1. **FAUZI bin ISNAN**, with the decision of Appellate Court of Jakarta, 04/Subv/Pid/90/PT.DKI dated 26 March 1990, who had been sentenced to twenty years in prison.
2. **SUDARSONO, alias MASDAR**, with the decision of Appellate Court of Jakarta 05/Subv/Pid/90/ PT.DKI dated 20 April 1990, who had been sentenced to seventeen years in prison.
3. **FADHILLAH, alias SUGITO bin WIRYOPERWITO**, with the decision of the Tanjungkarang District Court 160/Pid/B/Subv/1998/PN.TK dated 30 April 1990, who had been sentenced to life in prison.
4. **TARDI NURDIANSYAH**, with the decision of Tanjungkarang District Court 102/Pid/B/Subv/ 98/PN.TK, dated 21 December 1989, who was sentenced to seventeen years in prison.
5. **SUGENG YULIANTO, alias SUGIMIN**, with the decision of Tanjungkarang District Court 161/ Pid/B/Subv/1998/PN.TK dated 7 November 1989, who was sentenced to life in prison.

6. **RIYANTO**, with the decision of Tanjungkarang District Court 191/Pid/B/Subv/1998/PN.TK, dated 4 January 1990, who had been sentenced to life in prison.

7. **HARIYANTO YUSUF**, with the decision of Tanjungkarang District Court 102/Pid/B/Subv/1998 dated 6 November 1989, who was sentenced to life in prison.

8. **FACHRUDDIN, alias SUKIRNA**, with the decision of Tanjungkarang District Court 193/Pid/B/Subv/1998/PN.TK, dated 21 December 1989, who was sentenced to life in prison.

9. **ZAMZURI bin MUHAMMAD RAJI**, with the decision of Tanjungkarang District Court 145/Pid/B/Subv/1998/PN.TK, dated 25 October 1989, who was sentenced to life in prison.

10. **MUHAMMAD MUSHANNIF**, with the decision of Tanjungkarang District Court 194/Pid/B/Subv/1998/PN.TK, dated 20 December 1989, who was sentenced to twenty years in prison.

11. **ARIFIN bin KARYAN**, with the decision of Tanjungkarang District Court 195/Pid/B/Subv/1998/PN.TK, dated 8 December 1989, who had been sentenced to fifteen years in prison.

12. **ABADI ABDULLAH**, with the decision of Tanjungkarang District Court 196/Pid/B/Subv/1998/PN.TK, dated 19 December 1989, who had been sentenced to twenty years in prison.

13. **MUNJAENI**, with the decision of Tanjungkarang District Court 187/Pid/B/Subv/1998/PN.TK, dated 30 October 1989, who had been sentenced to twenty years in prison.

14. **SHOLIHIN**, with the decision of Tanjungkarang District Court 53/Pid/B/Subv/1998/PN.TK, dated 25 August 1989, who had been sentenced to thirteen years in prison.

15. **SRI HARYADI**, with the decision of Tanjungkarang District Court 163/Pid/B/Subv/1998/PN.TK, dated 30 October 1989, who had been sentenced to life in prison.

Their release met with a happy response. The Minister for Transmigration and Resettlement, A.M. Hendropriyono, was also happy to welcome them to the Muhajirin Mosque within the Ministry of Transmigration and Resettlement office. In their meeting of thanks, which was covered widely by the local media, A.M. Hendropriyono said that all Islamic political prisoners would be released in quick fashion based on the principle of reconciliation. They were not criminals, thieves or robbers. They were imprisoned due to politics and a misunderstanding of government policy.

Regarding their release, reconciliation was seen as a movement that appealed to the hearts of the government and the public. The Ministry of Transmigration, said Hendro, intended to accept responsibility for the political prisoners, who were mostly poor. They had the same right to be treated as other transmigrants, he said.

All of this has now passed. The settlement of the Talangsari case through reconciliation has become a reality. Those who were previously enemies have now come together. The stronger ones helped the weaker ones. Those who were unemployed are employed. Those who were looking to open businesses sought capital.

In fact, not everybody has been satisfied by the outcome. There will always be those that doubt. There will always be those that want too much. There will always be those that do not want the dispute settled. But in this case, we should be reminded to take wisdom from the commandment of God with regard to ending anarchy.

Those from both sides had dead in the battlefield. It was not a matter of winners and losers, since the only winner was the truth.

Reconciliation, if properly communicated, could become the solution to the present socio-political conflicts in Indonesia. We should strive to settle these matters in only one way: by referring to His rule!***

18

CLOSING

DEMOCRACY legalizes the right to live equally in a public that has diverse opinions. In reality, there will always be a conflict of opinion. But as long as there is an awareness that diversity is good, then there will be benefits. When diversity is not respected, it can lead to sporadic outbursts of violence.

The Lampung case can be considered the climax of the various upheavals described in this text. During the New Order, there were many cases in which sporadic violence took place among communities. What is of concern is that the violence sometimes took place because of Islamic idealism.

There are two basic elements that we sometimes ignore. These elements often lead to national tragedies in this country. The first is human ego, and the second is ideological fanaticism. Both can be dangerous in making friction between the Islamic community and the state. Those elements always appear in the various cases of political violence in Indonesia.

Human Egos

Egocentrism is a factor in each individual. This is what distinguishes us from God's other creatures. Besides egos, humans also need social orientation. This means that along with egocentrism, we also need societies in which we can participate.

Human beings must have both. The problem is which should be stronger: egocentrism or social orientation? Though humans have the freedom to determine who he or she will become, the best human being is the one that understands himself and determines what attitude he should take. This is because the line between egocentrism and social orientation is very thin and often uncontrollable.

The human identity is not easily identified. However, human actions are visible and cannot be negated. Sooner or later, one will identify a person's true nature. Warsidi's group from the Talangsari III hamlet used to say that whatever existed on Earth was the property of God. Therefore, they felt that they had the right to steal crops around the Cihideung complex because it was owned by God. They also said that whoever did not follow their brand of Islam was an infidel. This included those from the government who did not support them.

In actuality, such actions and attitudes can be classified as individualistic and egotistical. This was certainly the case when Warsidi rebuffed the summons by the Way Jepara sub-district chief. The best government comes from the clerics and the worst clerics come from the government, he said when he received the summons.

Ideological Fanaticism

Ideology never dies. Conflict in political life is always motivated by ideological diversity. It looks like Indonesia has been subject to various great ideological conflicts stemming from Nationalism, Communism, and Islam. As a nation, we have collectively experienced violence in the name of ideology. Just after the violence of the colonial era, the war of independence broke out and continued until the end of the Japanese era. Our parents discussed the basis of independence. The flag of the republic was to be the only unifier of the various ideologies when it came to formulating the basis for a state.

However, when the country was trying to uphold the flag, it was again invaded by the Dutch and violence broke out once more. People were shot dead, grenades were tossed, people were thrown from moving vehicles with their hands tied. That is why we have come to acknowledge violence as much as we acknowledge our own family. That includes those who live far from the cities. Villages are normally peaceful. But many people speak in depressed tones when they talk of living in villages when they were under siege by DI guerrillas or when they were in Madiun and attacked by the communists. We were fighting to be independent, but we were still fighting each other, burning down houses, having children cry in fear, and screaming at each other. All of this was done in the name of ideology taken to fanatical extremes.

In 1955, the country for the first time had an experiment in democracy. Ideological diversity would no longer be settled by weapons, but by the ballot box. The weapon of change would be the vote. But there emerged no dominant winner, and the legislative assemblymen fought among each other until their clashes were eventually settled by force.

During that period, ideologies became too rigid to face new realities. Soekarno's Marhaenism was unable to cope with the new reality of a growing middle and upper class, undercutting its ability to unify. Communism was unable to overcome the bankruptcy of a command economy and an authoritarian political system. And Islam could not be wielded by those who did not approve of a diverse country and its people. Still, this did not stop ideological fanatics. The New Order government came about and tried to eliminate all ideologies except the one they supported. The Islamic community, which was too indoctrinated against plurality, eventually began to see a clash between Islam and Pancasila. Those that supported Islam were seen as anti-Pancasila. At the same time, those that supported Pancasila were seen as turning their back on Islam.

In the Talangsari case and similar incidents, we can find such a clash of ideologies. To refuse Pancasila was like refusing paganism. This belief proved fertile grounds for Islamic fanatics. Having a state-supported ideology caused many splinter groups to push their existence through violent means. It even gave rise to a number of romantic Islamic heroes against the New Order. They built up fanatical followers who had little true understanding of Islam. The authorities were finally able to see how fanaticism was able to piggyback on true Islam when they raided the Mujahidin Fisabilillah community in Cihideung. As revealed in *Tempo* magazine, documents held by these groups stated, 'Islam is not as we have experienced it. We have come to be content with the NU version, the Muhammadiyah version, the Darul Hadist version. These are not true Islam.'

In the course of Indonesian history, many Islamic extremists have been called splinter groups. They are called splinter groups because they are isolated from mainstream organizations like NU and Muhammadiyah. The fact that they are splinter groups is reflected in their strict, revolutionary, and fundamentalist attitude. Such groups are extremely rigid and are not moderate in their judgement. It is often suspected that they deviate from the main religious teachings and faith. While not everything they say is wrong, not all of it is true.

It is a reality that all ideologies can become rigid if faced by recent realities. Ideological rigidity causes schisms and cracks in society. The community and the state become divided between traditionalists and modernists, between Islamic nationalists and secular nationalists, between those that want to cooperate and those that do not want to cooperate. In following a specific ideology, people come to believe that there is only one truth, while all others are opponents. Plurality must come to an end. Pluralism is regarded as unnecessary, filled with too many excuses. 'Truth' becomes reflexive.

Finding a Solution

Ideologies never die. However, Islam is not content only with ideological teachings. In reality, Islam intends to enlighten close-minded fanatics. To those with a closed mind, the community should eliminate all those who are secular, who do not abide by the same religion. Islam is even marginalized from the national political stage. However, education has opened opportunities to be on that stage. An objective—not subjective—way of thinking is required.

Islam is everywhere. It can be found among people with all kinds of careers, even in the bureaucracy and military. Islamic politicians and soldiers must end the notion that politics is a manifestation of the struggle between Muslims and non-Muslims, between Islam and the state. Islamic leaders must enlighten their communities about improving their creativity and scientific achievements. The objective of social politics should no longer be a mere symbol, like trying to convert the nation into an Islamic state. Rather, the goal should be to maximize the leadership potential of all Muslims in order to give benefit to all humans who support justice and prosperity. There must be a consensus within our community to no longer apply violence to settle problems. Our Indonesia is now waiting for a wise solution that will make all of its citizens content.

Within one person can be a saint and a tyrant. It is best to support tolerance and national unity by improving science and technology, and by having a compromising spirit in accepting the best solution to let our nation escape from everlasting division and suffering.

That is reconciliation.***